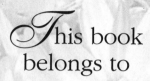

*T*his book
belongs to

_____

*May you know you are a
woman much loved, a woman
for whom God stopped
at nothing to pursue
your heart.*

When God Pursues a Woman's Heart

CINDI McMENAMIN

HARVEST HOUSE™ PUBLISHERS

EUGENE, OREGON

Cover by Koechel Peterson & Associates, Inc., Minneapolis, Minnesota

Some of the names have been changed to protect
the anonymity and privacy of the women who
shared their stories in this book.

WHEN GOD PURSUES A WOMAN'S HEART
Copyright © 2003 by Cindi McMenamin
Published by Harvest House Publishers
Eugene, Oregon 97402
www.harvesthousepublishers.com

Library of Congress Cataloging-in-Publication Data
McMenamin, Cindi, 1965-
    When God pursues a woman's heart / Cindi McMenamin.
    p. cm.
Includes bibliographical references.
    ISBN 0-7369-1131-6 (pbk.)
    1. Christian women—Religious life. 2. God—Love. I. Title.
    BV4527.M4328 2003
    248.8'43—dc21   2003003939

Printed in the United States of America.

03 04 05 06 07 08 09 10 /BP-KB/ 10 9 8 7 6 5 4 3 2 1

For the precious women of
South Mountain Community Church
in Draper, Utah—your lives are living proof that
God pursues our hearts!

Acknowledgments

I am so thankful to:

- The women who shared their personal stories for this book.

- My Mom—for teaching me of the love of Jesus when I was a little girl...and my Dad for showing me how that love can transform a life when I became an adult.

- My women's ministry leadership team and "inner circle" at Valley Bible Church—Robin Collier, Kendyl Goldston, Chris Castillero, Annie Courtney, and Natalie Barnhill—who share with me the romance of God's love.

- The Tuesday night prayer team at Valley Bible Church. Together, we saw God's heart and we witnessed Him coming through in mighty ways.

- My husband, Hugh, and daughter, Dana, for their support in the midst of late nights and long days of writing.

- My Harvest House family for enthusiastically embrac-ing this book and making it possible.

And I remain grateful to the Lord Jesus Christ...Bedrock under my feet, the Castle in which I live, my Rescuing Knight (Psalm 18:1 THE MESSAGE).

Contents

Come Rediscover the Romance

azing at the beautiful Cascade Mountains, my mind turned heavenward. I'd been told all my life that the God who created those mountains and breathed His majesty upon them still cared about the intimate details of my life.

"Where are you now, God?" I asked as the ache intensified in my heart. I'd just discovered that the one man I'd wanted all my life had married someone else.

"Do you have *anyone* for me?" I whispered through the pressure of mounting tears, fearing that my life would never hold the treasure I had hoped for.

In the stillness of that morning, I never heard a voice. But somewhere in the coolness of the breeze God's presence wrapped around me and assured me that He wasn't about to let me out of His sight or out of His heart. He convinced me that day that *He* was the One for me…and I was about to experience the romance of my life! Looking back at that morning, and the way pain had prepared my heart to come unreservedly to Him, I wondered if He had been waiting for that day all of my life.

You are My beloved, He seemed to whisper that morning through the cool breeze over the mountains, and into the hallway of my heart.

His Words, recorded in Scripture thousands of years ago, resonated with new life and spoke directly to the hollow within me: *"I have loved you with an everlasting love...I will call you back as if you were a wife deserted and distressed in spirit....For a brief moment, I abandoned you, but with deep compassion I will bring you back...."*[1]

I lifted my eyes upward to the God who knew me by name and was waiting for my return. And that day, a commitment was sealed deep in my heart to a Love I knew would never let me down. My circumstances didn't change that day. But Irresistible Love broke through, and I haven't been the same since.

The Creator and Sustainer of Life not only loves you, but longs for you to understand the depth of His pursuing love.

That morning in the mountains represented one day in many that I have stood in the silence of pain and asked God where He was and if He still cared. I came that day as a single woman, fearful for my future. I came again years later as a wife who was lonely in love. I came once as a daughter needing a Daddy. And I came just recently as a mother, needing wisdom and grace to raise a daughter who is so much like me. I still come today, when I'm tired and worn out, when I need to know I'm treasured, when nothing in the world will satisfy. But mostly I come when that ache deep within calls me to return to the precipice of encountering His love once again. Each time I come to that precipice, I find something more about Him that takes my breath away.

I know you've been there, too...on that precipice of wondering if God is really there, if His love is real, if He still cares despite what's happened in your life. I know you, too, have cried over lost love or lost opportunity, missed children or missed parents, broken hearts and broken dreams, a life that went awry.

But the Voice that penetrated my heart and reminded me that I was His beloved watches and waits for the opportunity to connect with *your* heart as well. Can you imagine that? God Almighty—who is *infinite*—wants to have a personal and *intimate* relationship with you. The Creator and Sustainer of Life not only loves you, but longs for you to understand the depth of His pursuing love.

From the moment God fashioned mankind in the Garden at the beginning of time, to the day He will rescue us and usher us into New Jerusalem, our Maker has been demonstrating His undying love for us. This powerful God who created all things is also a tender God who sustains all things.

Throughout the pages of this book, I want you to recognize how this God who is age-to-age the same communicates His pursuing love to you in ways you might not realize. Ways you can so easily miss. You see, sometimes He stops us with breathtaking beauty as a reminder of what He created for us. Other times He provides for us, but we don't recognize it was Him. He may, at times, pursue us like a Lover desperate for our affection. Or hold us close to His heart like a Daddy comforting a child. There are times He cheers us on when we need encouragement. Sometimes He speaks in a shout to protect us, sometimes in a gentle whisper. But always tenderly, wooing us to His heart.

Have *you* heard His voice lately? Have you seen a glimpse of how He pursues *your* heart?

If your answer is no, then I understand. I think we, as women, often reach a plateau in our relationship with God where we find it difficult to go deeper, to really feel His presence with us or know beyond a doubt that He is pursuing our hearts every moment of every day. A friend of mine who is a chiropractor, clinical nutritionist and counselor says we as women have been so conditioned to respond to medication, to treatment, to something we can feel, that we no longer know how to sense God personally. So have we, as women, lost the romance of a relationship with God? Have we lost that ability to live by faith, to listen for His voice, to look for Him—and "see" Him—in everything?

"We haven't *lost* the romance of the relationship," my doctor-friend says. "Most of us have never *found* it.

"God has become to so many of us like a chair in the room," she continued. "The chair is always there so we pretty much don't notice it anymore...not until we really need it."

My friend, if that is *your* experience with God, don't settle for it any longer. God is *not* a piece of furniture in the room. He is not just part of the air, or something as predictable as a chair. He is the living, breathing Presence who inspires us, the Father who protects us, the Provider who comes through for us. And He is the Pursuer of our hearts.

What is it about a woman's heart that He pursues? Perhaps it is our desire to be known completely and to be loved deeply. Maybe it's our nature to nurture and care for another. Perhaps it is the way we become so vulnerable with those to whom we give our heart. Or maybe it's just our desire to be romanced with all of our heart. I believe

God uniquely made us that way, and therefore He longs to not only be the One to ultimately fulfill us, but also to experience the pleasure that our love and devotion can bring Him.

Just as God made man in His image and wants to convey His might and strength through him, He made woman in His image as well, to reflect His softer side, to represent the side of Him that nurtures and notices, that gives love and receives it, that is tender, caring, and compassionate. God longs to make Himself known to man by being his strength, his confidence, his Father to imitate. And I can't help but feel that God wants to make Himself known to woman by being her Hero, her Provider, her Intimate Ally. Does God not delight as we wait for Him to *come through,* as we look to Him to *rescue,* as we long for *His* love to make us whole and as we dream of *His* love to one day sweep us away? In His eternal plan to create us and then redeem us, He is our White Knight, our Warrior determined to rescue us from prison, our Redeemer who wants to buy us back—not just for our salvation, but for His delight. We are His mission, His beauty to rescue, the object of His love and the pursuit of His heart.

No matter what the first part of your life looked like, no matter who else you've loved or how you've lost, no matter how you've sinned or suffered or slandered Him...Irresistible Love continues to come after you as well. Through the pages of the Bible—His love letter to us—we read of how He created us, the mission He has to rescue our hearts, the price He paid so we could be His. Against insurmountable odds, He has valiantly come through. No love on this earth could compare to the one He has so boldly yet tenderly, so methodically yet recklessly, shown toward us. Toward *you.*

So, if you're longing to experience God's touch in the still of the night, longing to hear His whisper in a soft breeze, longing to see His love for you in the gentle rain, it's time for you to experience that kind of love. It's time for you to take the adventure that will open your eyes and ignite your heart and sweep you off your feet. It's time to rediscover the romance of a relationship with God.

So, come with me, tender heart, through the pages of this book, to look upon this Lover of your soul who will stop at nothing to win you. Come see the softer side of God. Marvel at the mightier side of God. Wonder at the mysterious side of God. Come feel the gentleness that reminds you of the One who woos you to experience love like you've never known it before. And know what it's like to be completely and irresistibly swept off your feet.

For truly amazing things happen when God romances your heart.

Your Maker Who Fashioned You in Love

Have you ever wondered what was going on in God's mind when He fashioned woman thousands of years ago in the limitless beauty of paradise?

It must have been an adventure for Him, a special undertaking, a precious moment in which He performed His last, crowning act of creation. I like to think it went something like this:

"Come here," God whispered to Adam as He roused him from his sleep. "I have a surprise for you."

The Maker could barely contain His excitement as He wooed the man to a corner of the Garden where lush green grass and tall weeping willow trees hid His "surprise."

"I made her for you," the Maker said, and backed slowly away.

She emerged slowly from behind the curtain-like branches and leaves of the willow. Her eyes wide with anticipation and wonder, she was the essence of beauty... the epitome of wonderful, unanticipated surprise.

Adam couldn't believe his eyes! She was a perfect replica of him, yet different. Softer. Smoother. More elegant and wonderful with every curve. Her skin glistened in the sunlight. Her eyes connected with his and seemed to see right through to his soul. She smelled far better than the roses. She was beautiful. And she was...his?

Adam stood there, speechless.

And the Maker knew all that the man wanted—but didn't know how—to say.

There would be many times like that, the Maker smiled to Himself...but just wait...

She smiled, knowingly, as she looked from the man to the Maker and back to the Man again. She knew, too, all that Adam wanted—but didn't know how—to say.

The Maker beamed with pride. *She is made in My image.* She will discern your thoughts, she'll know what you're about to say and...yet watch....there....she will know what to say with a touch of her hand, a look in her eyes, a smile on her lips.

Harmony. Perfect harmony. Man and woman...together.

She was perfect. The man was whole. And the Maker was proud. Creation was complete. The Garden was more beautiful than it had been before. The lilies danced on the water. The birds chirped in the trees and the sun set on the Garden, causing it to glow, iridescent.

Finally, the man spoke.

"She's wonderful, too wonderful," he said, part exclaiming to his new bride, part praising his Maker, who grinned.

"Is she...mine?"

The Maker's heart skipped a beat. Of course He made her for him. But could man love her in the way she was created to be loved? Would man hold her the way God Himself longed to?

"Yes," the Maker said, "she's yours." *Hold her heart carefully, she is so precious,* He almost added, but didn't need to. It was clear Adam loved her completely.

"I will call her woman," the man said, looking directly into the eyes of this one he now loved, "because she came from man."

God walked slowly away, the lush grasses parting then closing again as He breezed through—as if to close the curtain on the two who would soon become one flesh.

The Maker sighed deeply as the wind from His nostrils blew through the trees in a presence-of-God satisfaction.

> *They wanted to know about God and everything else instead of living and experiencing the wonders of life He offered as they trusted and obeyed.*

They will know My love by the love they experience with one another, the Maker must have thought as He walked through the Garden. Then slowly He turned and looked toward the grasses where they would spend long hours exploring and enjoying each other's perfect bodies.

"Drink deeply of each other," He whispered. And as He walked away, leaving them to the beauty and quiet of the Garden, glowing at sunset, He could feel their smiles, sense their worship, and hear their praise.

❀ ❀ ❀

As the sun lit Eden in early morning, God walked through the Garden, smiling as He heard her giggling. Her laughter was music to His ears. She was sheer innocence and beauty. How He loved to watch her. How He loved the allure she held and the way her heart had captured Adam's, just as He had intended.

And the way she expressed herself…so intently, so poetically. She so unreservedly gave her heart to her husband and her Maker. *Oh, if it could last forever*, the Maker must have thought. But things were about to change….

🌿   🌿   🌿

In the cool of evening, God walked slowly through the Garden, His Spirit wind rustling through the trees. His heart was heavy. The day had come. And the Garden— and life as they knew it—would never be the same again.

Why did she do it? He must have thought. *I gave her everything. How could she possibly want more? How could she think I was withholding something from her? Didn't she trust Me? Didn't she trust that no good thing would I with-hold from her as she continued to walk uprightly before Me? Didn't she know she was the apple of My eye, that I had given her everything she needed? Yet, somehow, it was not enough.*

They had eaten of the forbidden fruit. They had chosen the tree of knowledge over the tree of life. They wanted to know *about* God and everything else instead of living and *experiencing* the wonders of life He offered as they trusted and obeyed.

The Maker's thoughts turned to anger. *How could the man let her do it? I gave her to him to protect, to oversee, to keep from evil. Why didn't he stop her? Did he desire her approval more than Mine? Was breaking My heart easier than breaking hers? Now they will have to leave, and I can no longer walk and talk with them as I once did.*

Adam…Eve…you are so far away! His heart cried out in anguish.

He came to the bushes where He knew they were hiding—*hiding* in this place where they were fashioned to live freely and unashamed.

"Adam, where are you?" the Maker asked in His gentle fatherly voice, waiting for His child to confess.

The couple emerged from the grasses where days earlier they had known only joy. The once-glorious creatures now looked stark and ashen and ashamed in the dusk, groping for covering in the leaves.

"You have disobeyed Me," the Maker spoke firmly. "You have rebelled against My orders. You have taken what I kept from you for your protection. Now you will clearly know, throughout your lives, why I had forbidden it." His voice must have quieted as He sadly ordered them to leave the Garden and live with the consequences of choosing their way over His.

The earth was cursed. Adam and all men after him would have to work hard to obtain the produce of the land. Eve and her daughters throughout time would live in the shadow of a man who was fallen. And because they now knew sin, they would have to leave the Garden. But not until their Maker clothed them.

Walking through the Garden again, this time not to fellowship with the couple, but to provide a covering for them, God sought a way for them to live in their nakedness and shame. He killed two animals, which He had shaped earlier for their pleasure, and clothed the couple with the beasts' skins.

The fur was warm, much better than the leaves, Adam and Eve thought. But the cost of sin was death to the animals and, eventually, to them. The couple sadly realized they would die one day as a result of their sin, and the pattern of death was set in motion for all of mankind. Disobedience to God, and choosing their way over His, ended up costing them paradise and their immortality. And God knew their sin would eventually cost Him *so much more*.

With a heavy heart, God pointed the way out of the Garden.

The sullen couple, with heads hanging low, walked out the garden gate and into the barrenness of the world where thorns and thistles were beginning to grow, where they would have to build their own shelter, labor for their own food, and protect their own skin. And as they walked, the Maker's hands remained outstretched.

The pain pulsed at the Maker's heart as He watched them go. And the same hands that were outstretched, pointing the way *out* of the Garden, would one day stretch across a splintery wooden cross, pointing the way *back* to the Garden...back to paradise...back to His side forever.

One day, He must have thought as they walked farther, *one day, I will hold you close to My side again. One day it will be possible. And one day, you will know Me fully and completely and perfectly...as you briefly knew each other.*

But for now, His heart would have to wait....

ℛesponding to the ℳaker's ℋeart

Eve lost Paradise because she believed God was withholding something from her. When have *you* felt God was withholding something from you?

Look at Psalm 84:11. If you are seeking God and walking uprightly, what might be the reason He is "withholding" something from you?

Have you ever considered that all the things you love about being a woman were designed by God, Your Maker? It was His idea that you shine, that you laugh, that you radiate with beauty. Yet it is our sin that causes us instead to be imperfect, unworthy, ashamed.

Think about who you would be in a perfect, sinless world. That is who you were created to be. And you can get a glimpse of that now, through the cleansing and completeness of the saving grace of Jesus Christ. (If you don't know what it means to be cleansed and complete in Christ, see "Giving Him Your Heart" on page 213.)

Dream with God, for a minute, about who and what you were created to be, and who you can be today with His righteousness in your life:

Lord, You made me a _____
woman with _____ and
_____ to offer all who would
come in contact with me. Help me to radiate
that _____ through Your Spirit
that can make me whole and clean. I want to
be seen, through Your eyes and through the
world's eyes, as a woman who _____
for Your glory and delight.

What thoughts and feelings cross your mind and heart
as you consider that someday you can experience God in
a way that two perfect, sinless people experienced and
enjoyed each other in the Garden?

🌹 🌹 🌹

A Prayer from the Heart

Lord, I will trust You no matter where I am
in life and what I'm going through. I will be
satisfied with what You have given me in Your
goodness and grace. Thank You for designing
me to live in relentless joy. Thank You for
seeing to it that I will again. I look forward to
the day I will know You as You intended.

A Caring Creator Who Longs for Your Return

God must have felt lonely the first evening He walked through the Garden alone. The man and his wife, expelled from the Garden because they chose to follow sin, would no longer be able to live in the lush beauty of paradise, communing freely with Him...at least not for a long time. The place that once rang with laughter and joy now bore only silence.

But there was a deeper silence—one that troubled both the woman and her Maker. Eve, who had once so freely conversed with God, now seemed so distant. She was distracted by the physical and emotional pain she now endured, by the fact her body was now slowly aging, by the full awareness of paradise lost. She couldn't focus on the Maker as easily. She had work to do, alongside her husband, to get food for her family to eat. She had sons to care for, to comfort as they cried, to ease their discomfort in their harsh surroundings. Sometimes it was easier to not think about what they once had in the Garden. After all, she couldn't talk to God, face to face, as she once did. The intimacy was gone. She could barely remember what it was like to look straight at His holiness, to look straight into His eyes.

But it was her Maker who longed for the intimacy of their conversations even more. He missed the way her eyes would sparkle as she walked in the Garden with Him and poured out her heart about all that she saw and felt. Although she had Adam, there was something more complete and full in her conversations with God and she knew that. Her Maker knew her on the inside and Adam still had to guess what she was feeling. Her God knew what to say, and Adam was still learning. God was her Husband in a way that Adam never could be. Eve missed that. So did God.

If only she had not chosen something else over Him. If only she hadn't chosen sin. If only she had remained in the Abundant Life, the Perfect Paradise He created for her.

Eve had children now, and a husband who worked hard. A husband who tired easily. Who became irritated. Who cried out in bursts of anger as he tilled the rock and weed-ridden soil. She had seen his perfect side. Now she had him in all his imperfection as well.

And what about what Adam had seen of her? He had seen her perfect and flawless beauty. Now she was imperfect, aging, slowly dying since the day she left Eden. Those days in paradise seemed so long ago, almost like a distant dream. Yet the constant ache of regret reminded her that her loss was painfully real.

She knew her Maker still loved her. He could never run out of love for her. He had fashioned her with His hands. She was precious to Him. How her heart pulsed within her as she reminded herself that there was still One who saw her as she was intended to be...who knew her on the inside...if only she could be up close with Him again.

If only...

‹ ‹ ‹

Have you ever considered how brokenhearted God must have been when His loved ones chose independence from Him over paradise? Yet Pursuing Love determined not to let them go. Even though Adam and his wife now lived in a harsh, cold world, ruled by sin, God was determined to woo His loved ones back to His arms—the closest they could get to heaven while still on earth.

So often, God's creatures curse Him when life gets tough, forgetting that it was our decision, way back then, to live life without Him. And as a result of our decision, pain and sickness are now a part of life. Hardship and heartache are now inevitable. It is the world we live in; it is the world we ultimately chose.

Yet, God did not write us out of the picture when He drove us out of the Garden. The plan of redemption through Jesus was already in the works, because His father-heart was longing for a way to get us back to His side.

Throughout His Word, God describes His tender father-heart toward His people, Israel, and toward those of us today who have submitted our lives to Him. He describes the tenderness that still extends toward us, even though we've long since forgotten the intimacy of living by His side in the Garden. In Hosea 11:3-4, God speaks to His people in the imagery of a father bending down to pick up a child and hold him against His cheek:[2]

> *It was I who taught [my child] how to walk,*
> *leading him along by the hand. But he doesn't*

know or even care that it was I who took care of him. I led [him] along with my ropes of kindness and love. I lifted the yoke from his neck, and I myself stooped to feed him (NLT).

The God of our hearts still stoops to feed us, still reaches down from on high to rescue when we call to Him.[3] The relationship was broken by us, not Him. His hand still extends.

Heaven cannot be found here on earth. It waits for us in the place where His arms still extend—in the invitation of His intimacy and love.

Yet how His heart must break when He sees us continue to grope along in this world, forgetting the intimacy our ancestors once shared with Him in the Garden of His love.

"How can I give you up?" He says in Hosea 11:8 (NLT). "How can I let you go?...My heart is torn within me, and my compassion overflows."

Like a parent longing to rush in to help the child who insists on doing his own thing, God often waits until we recognize our frailty and ask for His help.

Listen to more of the pleas from His heart for His people who have gone astray:

The LORD did not choose you and lavish his love on you because you were larger or greater than other nations, for you were the smallest of all nations! It was simply because the LORD loves you, and because he was keeping the oath he had sworn to your ancestors. That is why the LORD rescued you with such amazing power from your slavery under Pharaoh in Egypt. Understand, therefore, that the Lord your God is indeed God. He is the faithful God who keeps

> *his covenant for a thousand generations and*
> *constantly loves those who love him and obey*
> *his commands* (Deuteronomy 7:7-9 NLT).

He constantly loves us. Let Him count the ways: He stores our tears in a bottle,[4] binds up the brokenhearted,[5] and cares to count each hair on our heads.[6] And He will restore us again to paradise...but *His* paradise, not ours.

As women, we look for paradise here on earth in restful and relaxing vacations, the warmth of family relationships, short-lived love affairs, high-priced homes with scenic views, food that will delight our taste buds and satisfy our stomachs, and careers that feed our egos and promise to satisfy. But heaven cannot be found here on earth. It waits for us in the place where His arms still extend—in the invitation of His intimacy and love.

What about you? Where are you searching for heaven? Can you sense a residue of Eden that is still on *your* heart?

Author John Eldredge says our desire for beauty, adventure, and intimacy are lingering desires from paradise lost: "We were made to live in a world of beauty and wonder, intimacy and adventure all our days."[7] Our frustration, then, at heartache, pain and suffering, struggling to attain perfect love, and striving for a more fulfilling relationship with God is to be expected because "this isn't the way it was supposed to be."

Our former address was Paradise, Eldredge contends. So how could we ever be content with the imitations of this world? We can try to find heaven on earth, but we'll always be disappointed, always reminded that there is really *so much more.* Since we were made for Eden, we must live frustrated without it. But you and I *can* return to the closest thing on earth that resembles heaven: Irresistible Love, Himself.

When my husband, Hugh, visited the remote jungles of Papua New Guinea, he observed something peculiar and wonderful about the Iteri people. These tribesmen, in a church established years earlier by American missionaries, were a people obsessed with heaven. When Hugh—a white man from America who was schooled in the knowledge of the Scriptures—came to speak at the Iteri church, the natives bombarded him with questions, but not about doctrines or dispensations, interpretations or translations. They wanted to know more about heaven!

Lon, the American missionary to the Iteri people, attempted to explain to my husband the people's obsession with heaven. Because the Iteri dealt with so much suffering, saw so many of their loved ones die, and had such a high mortality rate, the life to come was all they really cared about.

How that must touch our Creator's heart—to know that somewhere in this world, some of His loved ones long to come back home.

When my husband recounted to me the Iteris' questions, my heart grieved over my own contentment with this earth to the detriment of my longing for heaven. Why isn't heaven all I think about? Why do I not long to be in His presence, to be away from the pain of this world, to be complete and whole, and by His side as I was created to be? In what ways have I gotten used to this world and forgotten my *real* home? What cheap substitutes for heaven have I settled for?

Oh, to have a longing to be with the Maker of our hearts...to long for Him as much as He longs for us. Today, I've noticed that my longing for heaven is directly proportionate to my longing for Him.

Do you yearn to return to the Garden for which you were created? Do you long to live alongside the Maker of your soul in the freedom and fullness that is promised? Would you like to see those bottles of your tears and read those thoughts He has recorded of you over time?

You can, because heaven exists. And it awaits you like a hometown beckoning your return. But while you're still on earth, you can have the next best thing to paradise—a life lived in the arms of Irresistible Love. Throughout this book, we'll discover how.

Recovering
Paradise Lost

Are you a woman who believes she's found heaven here on earth? In other words, do you long for the day you will enter eternity, or is something else making you want to stay here?

List the things you find yourself longing for more than heaven itself:

What about your heavenly Father's presence resembles paradise? List the qualities by which you have come to know your Maker, your Redeemer and the Pursuer of your heart:

A Prayer from the Heart

Forgive me, Lord, for rarely considering how *You* felt when Adam and Eve lost paradise. How Your heart must still ache to hold Your creation close! Draw me into a longing to be with You and You alone so I can experience paradise in Your loving arms. As Your Word says, "Draw me after You and let us run together!" (Song of Solomon 1:4 NASB). May my perspective, daily, be one of running to You and looking to Your ways and words to make sense of my life in this world. Make this the prayer of my heart: "Keep me safe, O God, I've run for dear life to you. I say to GOD, 'Be my Lord!' Without you, nothing makes sense."[8]

Your Protector Who Sees and Understands

Hagar squinted as she looked up toward the sky. The sun was scorching in this portion of the desert and once she left this spring, she knew it could be miles before she found water again.

She looked at the long road ahead of her. Exhausted at the thought of walking a step farther, she crumpled to her knees and sat on the hard desert ground. Despair began to close in on her, and she fought the urge to collapse into tears.

Where am I going to go? she thought as she considered how far she had come already. *I can't go back now.* She hung her head as scenes from the past several years played through her mind. She had been a stranger in the house of her master, the well-known Abraham, when he purchased her as a teenager. She was scared and alone. But she finally began to feel at home when the master's wife, Sarah,⁹ took her under her wing. She became Sarah's maid and the lonely old woman eventually confided in her. They became best friends and talked about everything, especially plans for the heir God promised to give the elderly, childless couple. But after several years, Sarah's hope and enthusiasm for a baby began to wane...until the day she suggested that maybe the child could come from Hagar. The young woman couldn't imagine that she would be any part of a plan from the living God with such an important man like Abraham. Her? An Egyptian maid? A woman who had nothing? Still, the idea intrigued her.

Hagar was reluctant, at first, when Sarah gave her to the master as a second wife and instructed her to make love to him in hopes of conceiving a child. She had never known a man intimately before. And she had always imagined having a child with a man whom she loved. But these were her orders...and they were better than living out her life childless, like Sarah.

Abraham was distant, but tender for an old man. And Hagar conceived immediately. With new hope and life within her, she thought surely circumstances would change for her. *The mother of the long-awaited heir would certainly be treated with respect and dignity,* she thought. Perhaps now she would no longer be a maid. But when nothing changed concerning her status, Hagar began to resent Sarah...and refuse to do some of the tasks her mistress ordered. Today it all came to a head as Sarah spoke harshly to Hagar, ordering her to clean faster, lift things that were heavier, work harder than she ever had before, even though she was pregnant. *Enough!* Hagar said to herself with lips clenched tightly. She threw the linens to the floor, ran out of the house, and just kept running.

I'll never go back, Hagar thought as she now considered the woman who had once been her friend and the only man she had ever known. Sarah had betrayed her. She ran her hand over her protruding stomach. *What will become of the baby now?* she thought. She frowned in deeper despair. It was her baby—not just Abraham's.

Her insides ached and nausea came over her as she realized the only hope for an unwanted, pregnant runaway slave was to lay down and die. She closed her eyes and clutched her stomach, and hoped to die. But Pursuing Love wouldn't let her.

> *With tear-filled eyes, she could only manage a whisper that she knew He heard: "You are the God who sees me."*

Instead of the throes of death, a cool breeze blew over her, and she heard a gentle voice echo through the desert canyon.

Hagar, maid of Sarah, where are you going?

The Voice was commanding, yet compassionate.

Hagar bolted upright.

Who's there? she thought, but didn't dare ask. She trembled with fear, although something within her said there was nothing to be afraid of. This Voice, after all, had called her by name.

The Voice asked again, this time in a fatherly way: *What are you doing out here?*

"I'm running from my mistress, Sarah," Hagar said hesitantly as a fearful realization came over her. *Is it...? Could it be...the God of Abra...?* She threw herself back to the ground, face in the dirt, in fear for her life. But the Voice softened and a gentle breeze encircled the woman, as if to embrace her, blowing her dark black hair in a stream behind her.

The Voice continued to speak to Hagar, softly and gently, telling her things about herself that even she didn't know: She would have a son. His name would be called Ishmael. God had seen her misery and her fear. She was to go back home and submit to Sarah. And she was going to be okay.

As the young woman lifted her face off the ground, she realized she wasn't going to die in the desert. The gentle breeze enveloped her, bringing strength and joy to every fiber of her being. She closed her eyes and lifted her hands into the gentle blowing and relished in the cool wonder of heaven on earth...and a new hope in life.

As the breeze stilled and the voice stopped, Hagar longed for more. She searched for words to convey what her heart wanted to say to this God who knew her from the inside out. With tear-filled eyes, she could only manage a whisper that she knew He heard: "You are the God who sees me."

After a few moments, Hagar rose to her feet and turned a determined face toward the road back home. Minutes ago she had vowed never to go back. But now it was different. How could she not trust such a comforting voice? How could she not feel safe with the simple orders from One who understood? How could anything awful ever again happen to her now that she had heard from the God who sees her?

As Hagar started the long trek home, she didn't think about how Sarah might react when she returned. She didn't guess the severity of her master Abraham's disapproval when he learned she had run away. She didn't think about the long walk, or the heat, or her aching feet. She thought only of Pursuing Love. Love that understood her fear and her future. Love that had reached down from heaven to touch her pain. Love that wouldn't let her die in her despair. Love that was not just Abraham and Sarah's. Love that was *hers,* too.

Hagar gained more strength with each step she took toward home and she no longer noticed the weight on her back and legs. She felt as if she were being carried in the arms of Love. The Eyes that had seen her and watched her every movement were now guiding her home. Her tear-stained face now glowed with a new confidence. She was no longer Hagar the Hesitant, the second choice, the abused. She was Hagar the Loved and Protected. She wasn't carrying a baby that only *she* loved; she was carrying a child that God knew about, too.

Hagar's life-changing encounter with the God Who Sees gave her the strength to return home and bear the child. Irresistible Love intervened, swept her off her feet, and gave her the confidence to go on.

🌼   🌼   🌼

Have there been times when *you've* wanted to run...to get out of your situation, escape the boiling pot? Have there been times you felt like you'd rather die than face another day in your house, or with your husband, or in that pain or particular circumstance? Are you at times like Hagar the Hesitant, feeling second-choice, bitter at betrayal?

Is there not a God who sees *you* as well? And in those eyes that never turn away from you, isn't there a look that beckons you to stick it out, to keep your eyes on Him, to return and submit...and remind you that you will be okay?

Whatever you're running from, wait for the gentle blowing of His pursuing love to find you. Listen for that voice that asks "Why are you running?" and gain strength from the fact that you are a woman much loved: You live in the realm of a God Who Sees.

Returning to His Love

What are you running from right now? (It could be a physical or emotional situation or an obligation.) Tell the Lord, right now, realizing that He sees and understands:

In what way do you need to return to God and submit?

Choose a favorite verse from the Bible to remind you of your Protector. (You may want to choose from Psalm 32:7, Psalm 40:11, or Psalm 116:6.) Write it out below. Then, write a statement of your own about your Protector who sees and understands:

A favorite verse about my Protector:

A personal statement about my Protector:

🌹   🌹   🌹

A Prayer from the Heart

O Lord, You are the One who sees all. It comforts me to know that when no one else understands what I'm going through, You do. Help me to see the lesson within my situation. But more than that, help me to look closely enough at You to see Your irresistible, pursuing love. You truly are "the God who sees me" (Genesis 16:13).

Your Fulfiller of Dreams Who Can Do the Impossible

All Sarah wanted was to have a child. Was anything wrong with such a desire? Was that too much to ask from God? He had blessed her with so much...except the one thing she wanted most.

She had tried everything under heaven, even giving her maid, Hagar, to her husband, Abraham, hoping to have a child through her. But even that child didn't feel like a fulfillment of the promise.

Now she was 89 years old. Maybe God had forgotten. Maybe it was all a mean trick. Maybe it was all a mistake to hope in an impossible promise from a God she'd never seen.

But Sarah would soon find that the only mistake was her hesitation to believe the impossible!

One day two strange men came to talk with Abraham. They were strange in that Sarah had never seen or heard of anyone like them. They talked with authority, as if they knew everything about the couple. How was that possible if they had never met? Listening intently just outside

Abraham's tent, Sarah heard the strangers say something comical.

"When we return at this time next year, Sarah will have a son."

Me? Pregnant? In this old body? And by my husband, who is nearly a hundred years old? This was so absurd it was funny. And Sarah laughed to herself.

But the Promise Maker, on the other side of the tent, discerned her disbelieving heart.

"Why would Sarah laugh at such a thing?" he asked Abraham, in all seriousness. "Why would she say 'how can a woman my age bear a child?' Is anything too difficult for God?" (see Genesis 18:13-14).

Sarah was embarrassed for having laughed. Especially when she found herself pregnant a few months later. And just as the stranger had said, when he returned a year later, she was holding that baby in her arms.

Sarah and her husband called their new son Isaac, which means "laughter," because God had made an absurdly impossible promise come true. He had given a new baby to an old lady. And through that the joy of tiny feet, baby's cries, and youthful laughter blew into their household. Nothing is too difficult for God!

🌿   🌿   🌿

Stephanie knows what it's like to wait on God too. For years, she has put her hope in a principle from Proverbs 22:6: that if she trains her children in the way they should go, when they are old, they will not turn from it. Like many mothers, she has brought her children up in the knowledge of God and done all that is humanly possible to see them give their hearts to Jesus, but has still seen her children choose the path of rebellion. "But my God is faithful," she says with a light still in her eyes. "I waited a while to see this one come back," she said, pointing to her oldest daughter, Kellie, who sat with her in a Bible class one Sunday morning. "I may have to wait awhile longer for the others. Apparently God's timing is different than mine." Stephanie has not seen this principle from Scripture played out in all her children's lives, but she waits with hope in her heart. Her hope is not in a verse from God's Word, but in God Himself, who promises that He will work all things together "for the good of those who love him, who have been called according to his purpose" (Romans 8:28). She believes that a God who can give a 90-year-old woman a baby can also give a child back to a middle-aged mother when it appears there is no hope. Is anything too difficult for Him?

Have you, like Sarah, wanted something for so long that it seems an impossible dream? Have you, like Stephanie, held onto hope but not yet seen it realized? Do you wonder at times if God has forgotten a promise He may have made to you? Sometimes God waits so long to deliver on a promise that we begin to believe He has long since forgotten. But the question asked of Abraham must be asked of you as well: Is anything too difficult for the Lord? The God who asked that question to Abraham in all seriousness is the same God who later said, "With God all things are possible."[10] Do you believe that? If not, it's time to reacquaint yourself with the Maker and Fulfiller of Dreams, who makes the impossible come true. Scripture tells us that all the Lord's promises prove true. In Psalm 119:140, the psalmist said, "Your promises have been thoroughly tested; that is why I love them so much" (NLT). God's promises *prove true* even when they're put to the test by

> *He longs to hear you say with all confidence, "There is nothing too difficult for my God."*

you and me, people who so easily doubt and give up. Keep in mind, of course, that we're talking about actual promises, and not merely our desires or wishes.

What promises has He made to you? With your God, you can do the impossible, and with His help, you can see miracles realized. The God of miracles lives today, and He longs to hear you say with all confidence, "There is nothing too difficult for my God."

When my youngest brother, Steven, was in preschool, he would pose with his skinny little arms and pretend he was a strong, muscular man and sing about how his God is so great, so strong and so mighty, that there's nothing his God cannot do. How often we as children will sing of the mighty wonders of God, but when we get older, we begin to limit His power to just what we *think* He can do. Yet God is just as big today as He was when we were little children, and He is the same miracle-working God whose heart is set on showing us how He can beat the odds, come through, and prove that He is the God of the Impossible.

Do *you* need a God of the Impossible right now? Do you need to be reminded that all that He has is yours?[11] Do you really believe He will take care of what concerns you?[12]

Keep believing in that dream. Keep trusting in that promise. Begin to see God as your Hero who *will* come through even at the eleventh hour and even if it doesn't seem likely. A 90-year-old woman wasn't too old, in God's eyes, to start a family! Remember, He's eternal. He has all the time in the world...so if He's waiting, He must know something about the time you have left, too! So go ahead. Dare to dream that dream...especially if it's something He has clearly stated to you in His Word. God will never abandon His promises. In fact, He tells us not only will He fulfill what He has promised, but He will do it in a way that is "immeasurably more than we ask or imagine" (Ephesians 3:20). Now *that's* worth waiting for.

ℛelying on ℋis ℛromises

What promise from God have you nearly given up on because it's taken Him so long to bring it about?

Is this a clearly stated promise from God's Word? If so, write it out and pray it through:

What would it take for you to clearly say, "Nothing is too difficult for the Lord?"

Reflect prayerfully on the following promise from God:

> "The LORD will fulfill his purpose for me; your love, O LORD, endures forever—do not abandon the work of your hands" (Psalm 138:8).

A Prayer from the Heart

Lord, You are the Fulfiller of Promises. You are also One whose love endures forever. Thank You that as I wait for unfulfilled promises to be realized, I can rest in Your unfailing, all-enduring love. How good it is to know that even the writers of the Bible, at times, feared that You might "abandon the work of your hands." You created me and You know I am frail at times, so please bring about Your purposes in my life in Your fullness of time. Keep me joyful, Lord Jesus, with the hope of Your Word and Your love.

Your Provider Who Always Finds a Way

All his life, he'd wanted a child. Now God was asking him to give up his only son. *Selfish, greedy God!* Abraham could have thought as he headed up Mount Moriah with his 12-year-old son. But a mysterious trust in the Invisible Almighty caused Abraham to unquestioningly follow the order.

As he bound his son to the stack of wood, his heart must have torn in two: *Do it painlessly, Lord, take Him quickly... then bring him back to* me. But when Abraham lifted his arm to bring that sharp-edged knife down into his son's chest, God Almighty stopped Him, and said, "Now I know that you fear God, because you have not withheld from Me your son, your only son" (Genesis 22:12).

Then Abraham looked up and saw a ram caught in a bush—God's provision for the sacrifice so Abraham's son could live.

Why all the talk of sacrificing Isaac anyway? Was this a mean trick? Couldn't God see the heart of His friend, Abraham, and already know that he would be loyal? Why did Abraham and Isaac have to go through all this? Apparently God had a special appointment with Abraham to show him that He was Jehovah Jireh—"the LORD Will Provide." And the day He provided a ram to take the place of Isaac was a foreshadowing of the day He would provide a Lamb to die in our place someday—the Lamb of God, Jesus Christ.

He is the God who provides...in more ways than we can fathom. And perhaps Abraham would never have known that so clearly without preparing to sacrifice Isaac and experiencing firsthand how Pursuing Love intervened.

🌱   🌱   🌱

I suppose God does the same with you and me. He lets us go through "all of that" so that we will know, beyond a doubt, that He is the One who provides, in more ways than we can fathom.

Dorothy knew of this God who provides. She had believed in Him most of her life. But never were days more desperate than they were now. She and her husband, Larry, had moved from Oregon to Southern California in faith, hoping that a job awaited Larry. But the job never materialized. Through prayers and the kindness of good friends, they lived for nearly a year on next to nothing—by house-sitting, taking odd jobs here and there, and continually praying for work opportunities and blessings to get them by. Finally, a real estate job opened up for Larry, but this meant the couple would have to move

Once again, God had provided exactly what they needed, at the moment they needed it.

from their temporary residence with friends to a permanent place another 60 miles south. Not able to afford a moving truck, a friend loaned them one to make the move. Just 30 miles down the highway, the rear tire blew out on the borrowed truck. *Could things get any worse?*

After making several phone calls, they found a tire that would fit on the borrowed truck, and the store could deliver it to them the next morning. But it would cost $142. That was more money than the couple had, and they didn't feel they could impose upon friends any more than they already had. They prayed earnestly, asking God to somehow provide. Then Larry stayed on the road with the truck while Dorothy lodged with friends overnight. The next morning, before Dorothy got a ride back to Larry and the parked truck, she asked her friend to drive her by the last home where the couple had lived so she could check the mail one last time. In the mailbox was a card from some longtime friends in Larry and Dorothy's prayer group in Oregon. The note said the group had been praying for Larry and Dorothy and felt called to send them a little extra cash in case they had a need. Enclosed in the card was a check in the amount of $142! Once again, God had provided exactly what they needed, at the moment they needed it. That day, Dorothy and her husband not only moved to San Diego, but to a deeper trust in Jehovah Jireh, the Lord who provides. They learned He is a God of detail. A God of exact amounts at the precise time. A God who doesn't miss a beat or allow His people to go hungry.

🌿 🌿 🌿

In Psalm 145:14-16 we're told, "The LORD helps the fallen and lifts up those bent beneath their loads. All eyes look to you for help; you give them their food as they need it. When you open your hand, you satisfy the hunger and thirst of every living thing" (NLT).

Our God has been providing for His loved ones since the beginning of time. His Word tells us He will supply all our needs according to His riches in Christ Jesus (Philippians 4:19). He also makes it clear that it's our needs He will supply, not necessarily our *wants*. Bottom line is, if we truly need it, He already knows and has a plan in the works. After all, He was aware of our greatest need before we even realized it—our need for salvation. His diligence in providing for our greatest need gives us reason to be confident that our lesser needs will not go unnoticed by Him.

If this God who pursues your heart could provide a way for you to someday meet Him face to face, then surely He can provide whatever it is that you need today! In the midst of your need, remember what God has already provided. A God who withheld nothing to give us His Son surely will not withhold anything else good for His children.

What do *you* need God to provide for you right now? Will you trust the One who boasts of owning the cattle on a thousand hills?[13] Will you believe that He really *will* supply all your needs according to His riches in heaven?[14] Will you let Him be your Husband-Provider?[15] Remember, in His pursuing love, He will find a way to come through for you.

Trusting in His Provision

What are some of the things you worry about God not providing?

In Philippians 4:19, we are told God will supply all our needs according to His riches in Christ Jesus. We're also told in Matthew 6:26-30 that God provides for the flowers of the field and the birds of the air, so surely He will provide for us, whom He loves so much more. Tell God about the things that concern you and praise Him for His provision which is already promised:

Fill out the following, as a prayer to Jehovah Jireh, your Lord who provides:

> Lord, I'm often concerned about _____.
> Yet Your word says You will not only accomplish what concerns me, but You will supply *all* my needs according to Your riches in heaven. I will trust You by _____
> and _____ each time that I begin to worry about whether or not You will come through.

A Prayer from the Heart

Lord Jesus, why is it that I can trust You with my eternal life yet I have trouble at times trusting You with my everyday life? If You can take care of my soul and my eternal destiny, surely You can take care of whatever concerns me today. Thank You that You are able. Thank You for finding a way to make me Your own... even at such a painful price! Thank You for considering my needs dear to Your heart simply because *I* am dear to Your heart. May my trust in You during times of uncertainty endear me to Your heart all the more. I love You, my Jehovah Jireh, My Pursuer and Provider.

The Restorer Who Turns the Bitter to Sweet

*I*t was dark as Deb drove up to her empty house. Her husband was still out fishing, and she had just dropped off her youngest daughter at a play production. The family had been gone from the house since noon and it seemed eerie returning home with no one there and the outside light turned off. As Deb turned the key and opened the front door, she heard the sound of running water. Her worst fear was confirmed as her feet sunk into a river of water. The house was completely flooded!

Wading down the hallway, her shoes squishing through water up to her ankles, she found the source of the disaster: water was shooting out of her bathroom sink, up to the ceiling, and then overflowing onto the floor.

Fortunately, Deb knew where the main water valve was located—out in her front yard. But it was dark, she'd just had her nails done, and she couldn't shut off the valve. Frantically, she called her husband, who was now on his way home from his fishing trip. He talked her through the process, and at last she was able to shut off the water. But when Deb entered the house again, she was afraid to turn on a light switch. Would she be electrocuted? She knew she needed to see the extent of the damage, and she began to wonder what she had left on the floor throughout the house that would be ruined.

Suddenly, her blood ran cold—Karly's wedding dress! Her oldest daughter, Karly, was getting married soon, and her brand-new white wedding dress was hanging to the floor in her bedroom closet. What if it was destroyed? She quickly prayed that God would protect that dress.

When Deb's husband arrived home, he turned on the lights so they could see the damage. They waded through each room, groaning at what they saw. But upon entering Karly's room, they saw a blessing in the midst of the disaster. The water had stopped just a few feet short of the closet. It was the *only* area in the entire house that had been spared. The family praised God that, in the midst of the ruin, they had seen a sign of His grace.

But that was the first sign of many to come!

Within an hour of contacting their insurance company, a truck arrived with machines and hoses to suck up all the water. One by one, Deb's kids returned home, shocked at the scene they encountered. Sadly they watched as their furniture and bags of belongings were set out on the front lawn. The workers told them they needed to spend the night somewhere else.

By that time it was long past midnight. After calling every hotel in the area and being reminded it was Labor Day weekend, they found "no room at the inn." They wondered who they could call at such an hour. It was already early Sunday morning and Deb and Karly had to be at church around 7:30 A.M. to lead and sing on the church's worship team. They felt blessed when they realized there were five or six families in their church that they knew would welcome them over in the middle of the night. They ended up calling two of their closest friends, who responded with, "Of course…come on over."

Later that morning, Deb realized that the music she had selected several days earlier for that Sunday was about God's grace, and now she had a perfect illustration of how her family had seen God's grace in protecting Karly's wedding dress amid the flood and giving them friends they could impose upon in the middle of the night. What could have been a tired and difficult morning for her at church turned out to be a sweet time of sharing her testimony about God's goodness in the midst of grief.

The following day, the family checked into a local hotel conveniently located close to their home. They divided the family of five into two rooms, and although the rooms seemed like tight quarters, the family started seeing the blessings add up. There happened to be a heat wave in town that week and the hotel had a pool for guests to refresh themselves in—something Deb's family didn't have back at home. The hotel offered a continental breakfast every morning, which they all enjoyed, and because the hotel rooms didn't have kitchens, the insurance company provided the family with an allowance for meals, which meant they got to eat out nearly every night, a treat that they couldn't afford on their usual family budget.

"What the insurance people called an evacuation turned out to be a vacation," Deb fondly recalls. And eventually, they saw that what could have been a stressful situation (having to live with little in such a small space) turned out to become some of the best memories around a table that the family had ever experienced together.

For a while the family didn't have to cook, and a maid cleaned up their rooms every day. But pretty soon, the days turned into weeks, and eventually into months. The rooms seemed to get smaller, and everyone began missing their home. The wedding was approaching, and there was much to do and so little space at the hotel.

"The blessing in all this was that our family stayed close and amazingly, conflicts just didn't happen," Deb said. Everyone coordinated their shower schedules and they purchased a box of nose strips for those in the family who snored, so that the non-snorers wouldn't be kept awake.

"Instead of all of us going off to our separate areas of a house, we actually spent a lot of time talking together. The blessing of being in two rooms is that we reconnected as a family," said Deb.

God had to take them on a faith walk through the challenging circumstances to help them find the blessing.

When it was finally time to return to their home, the family witnessed an amazing transformation. Their old home, which they had lived in for 30 years and was in bad need of repairs, looked brand new! The walls shined with fresh paint, the flooring had been replaced, plush new carpeting greeted their feet. Even damaged furniture was either cleaned, refinished, or replaced.

"Each day that we were in the hotel, we grew more dependent on God, came to appreciate our family more, and learned to do without some things. All the time, He was preparing a place for us beyond anything that we could have thought or asked for," Deb said.

In His pursuing love, God, in essence, gave the family a brand-new home. But God had to take them on a faith walk through the challenging circumstances to help them find the blessing. Deb now recalls that what started out as an utter disaster turned into an utter delight. What started out as bitter, God was able to make sweet.

The Israelites experienced a water problem, too. In Exodus 15, we read that they had just seen God separate the waters of the Red Sea so they could walk across on dry land. They sang, with all their hearts, about the goodness of God—His provision, His wonders, and His ways. But a mere three days later, they forgot about the God who had commanded the waters to part and started complaining about another water problem. Moses had led them into the desert, where they were tired and thirsty. And the only water they found was bitter and stagnant.

"What are we going to drink?" they grumbled and complained.

Fortunately for them, God's response was loving. God showed Moses a piece of wood and told him to throw it into the water. When he did, the waters became sweet, and the people could drink.

But God was more interested in cleaning their hearts than the water. He told the Israelites to listen to His voice, do what was right in His eyes, and obey His commands. Then He added, "I am the LORD who heals you."[16] God wanted to heal His people's complaining spirits, their critical hearts, their doubting souls. What happened next takes my breath away: "Then they came to Elim, where there were twelve springs and seventy palm trees, and they camped there near the water."[17]

God took them to Palm Springs!

Isn't that just like a God who restores? When Deb found her house flooded, she thought she had lost everything. But God gave her so much more out of it. When the Israelites thought they were doomed to die of thirst, God ushered them to a place of refreshment and shade and let them camp near cool springs of water. I love this story, personally, because on days when I'm tired and needing a rest, I call my friend, Midge, and she arranges for us to take our daughters on the one-hour drive to Palm Springs and there we rest by the pools of the Desert Hot Springs Hotel while our girls play in the water. The statement about the Israelites at Elim is a visual picture that reminds me that when we call on God and trust Him, He ushers us to that place of rest and refreshment.

Are you in a desolate place? Are you thinking that nothing good is happening to you? Are you finding much to complain about and little reason to rejoice? God may be waiting to take you to Elim—the place of refreshment and restoration, the place of abundance and blessing. But the bridge from desolation to delight is placing your trust in God's healing and restoring love.

God, in His restoring love, desires that we be whole— physically, emotionally, and spiritually. And He wants to heal our doubting, complaining, unbelieving hearts. Yet we need to trust Him, seek Him, and let Him lead us. Jehovah Rapha—the Lord Who Heals—is waiting to change your bitterness into blessing, ready to turn your stagnant waters to sweet.

Yes, you *can* find Elim every day of your life. You *can* find that place of quiet trust when your situation looks bleak. You *can* eventually experience blessings from what was once thought bitter. You can find it…when you grab hold of the hand of Pursuing Love and let Him take you on a faith walk.

Believing in His Restoring Love

What situations in your life appear bitter right now?

Do you believe God can turn these sources of bitterness into blessing?

Give God the bitterness in your life (a complaining spirit? a situation you're not happy with? a grudge against a person?), and let Him turn it into something beautiful. Your trust in God's love and restoration is the only bridge from disaster to delight.

Can you recall some tragedies in your past that produced treasure? If so, list them here:

Those tragedies-turned-treasures are evidence of Pursuing Love at work. Thank Him for them.

❧   ❧   ❧

A Prayer from the Heart

God, I realize now that the things which appear ugly on the outside, until I let You transform me with them, can help create something beautiful on the inside of me. Thank You for the situations in my life that You have redeemed, the treasures You've brought from the tragedies, and the difficult times that have developed me into a person who can take a faith walk. Thank You for caring enough about me to take the situations in my life, even the bad ones, and turn them into evidences of Your pursuing, restoring love.

Your Redeemer Who Gives You a New Life

Paula desperately wanted to avoid God. Especially because her father—who was pretty much nonexistent in her life until she was a teenager—had "found God" and wanted her to find Him, too.

Why would she want anything to do with a father who had left her and a God who had anything to do with her father? Although she remembers praying to God as a child every night before bed, this God now seemed like someone she had no intention of knowing.

Paula spent her teenage years chasing after anything that would make her happy and that would make her father mad. At 16, she became pregnant by a boy who didn't even like her. At 23, she had two failed marriages, a five-year-old child, and a pile of baggage and bitterness that told her she didn't need anyone or anything anymore, least of all, God. But by the time she married her third husband and had her second and third children, she realized there was an emptiness in her life that couldn't be filled, and she grew increasingly concerned about her children's spiritual—or lack of a spiritual—foundation. Then, as if the family were being gently pushed to a place where they absolutely needed God, a devastating situation rocked all of them.

"It stemmed from my husband's addiction to pornography," Paula recalls. "I remember as if it happened this morning, kneeling beside my bed one day, sobbing, crying out to God that I didn't know how to handle this. I didn't know what to do. I had never been so scared in my entire life. Our family was potentially going to be ripped apart, and I knew that God was the only one who could get me through it."

Paula cried out to God and what happened next proved the presence of Pursuing Love. "My heart and life were broken, spilled out on the ground, and I was empty. I knew it would be a miracle if we survived. Yet God, in His amazing, incomprehensible way, reached down and lifted me up out of my pit of despair, of hopelessness, of devastation, and poured His love over me."

> "I am a chosen one of God and I know He loves me. Nothing about me is the same anymore."

God miraculously healed Paula's marriage and family and brought them to Himself. They started praying as a family, changed their lifestyle drastically, her husband sought personal accountability, and Paula learned firsthand the meaning of unconditional love and grace.

"All my life I believed God was too big and too busy for me, and now I was being told, from the Bible, that He loves *me*. He died for *me*. That blew me away. It was almost too much. It still makes me weep when I think of it in those simplest of terms."

Why did God intervene in her marriage in order to rescue Paula and redeem her life? Because she earned it?

Because God owed her? No, because Pursuing Love wouldn't let her go.

"My life isn't perfect now, but it is wonderful," Paula said, through tears, as she shared her story at her church's women's retreat. "I am a chosen one of God, and I know He loves me. Nothing about me is the same anymore."

Nothing ever is...when one encounters Redeeming Love.

Psalm 71 speaks of our lives as a testimony of what God has done for us, recounting His constant help from childhood to old age. Listen to the tender words about a God who knew you since your youth and redeemed your life in His sight:

> O Lord, you alone are my hope. I've trusted you, O LORD, from childhood. Yes, you have been with me from birth; from my mother's womb you have cared for me....My life is an example to many, because you have been my strength and protection (Psalm 71:5-7 NLT).

Now, look at this!

> Though You have made me see troubles, many and bitter, you will restore my life again; from the depth of the earth you will again bring me up. You will increase honor and comfort me once again....My lips will shout for joy when I sing praise to you—I, whom you have redeemed (Psalm 71:20-21,23).

Have you seen troubles in your life, many and bitter? Can you recall days when you wondered if there was a God around at all, let alone one who loved and cared for you? Have you wondered, at times, if *your* life was worth redeeming in God's sight?

Rahab may have wondered that, too. A well-known prostitute in the walled city of Jericho, she lived a hardened life. Who knows what drove her to sell her body to a man for a price? Yet something softened in this woman's heart the day two Israelite spies came to town. Hiding them on her roof, she lied to the authorities so the men could escape because she had heard of their God. Apparently she believed He was the Lord, and the only one who could not only save her life, but rescue her heart as well. She made the men swear to her that when they destroyed the city, they would spare her and her family's lives for her kindness to them.[18]

They did more than that. They brought her and her entire family out of the city before it was destroyed and made them a part of the nation of Israel.[19] God not only spared Rahab and her family, He gave her a new start...and a new lineage as well. God saw to it that this prostitute got a husband who loved her, had a son of significance, and became an ancestor of Jesus. In the first chapter of Matthew, which lists Jesus' ancestors, only four women's names are included in a genealogy of mostly men. One of them is Rahab. Not Rahab who had been the prostitute, but Rahab, who had become the wife of Salmon, mother of Boaz, and great-grandmother of King David. (Incidentally, the other three women mentioned in the genealogy of Christ are Tamar, a victim of incest; Ruth, a woman from the cursed nation of Moab; and Bathsheba, an adulteress. When God redeems a woman and restores her honor, He does it all the way!)

I love the way God redeemed Rahab and then gave her a new identity. No longer was Rahab a prostitute, the label her city had put on her, the label with which she identified herself. She became Rahab the wife and mother. Rahab the dignified. Rahab the chosen one. Rahab the honored woman in the bloodline of Christ.

What labels have you let the world put on you? I've been told I'm an adult child of an alcoholic. Yet God's Word tells me I'm a child of the King. Maybe you were labeled something derogatory in high school, a label that symbolized your life before you knew Christ. But if you're a Christian, God's Word calls you "a new creation," "saint," "righteous" in Him. Many women I know struggle with being called "enablers" in a codependent marriage. But God's word calls them "brides" of Christ. When we come to know Jesus in a personal relationship, God puts shiny new labels on us that tell our redemption story. His labels for us are so much better than the world's. His labels say "friend," "beloved," "heir of all that is."

At a retreat at which I was speaking a couple years ago, the worship team led everyone in a song called "My Redeemer Lives" just before the last session of the weekend. I couldn't help but notice one of the college-aged girls in the front row jumping up and down, tears streaming down her cheeks as she looked heavenward, hands raised high, and sang the words "My Redeemer lives, my Redeemer lives...." I didn't even need to ask. I smiled as I realized she was another one who had lived the redemption story, who had exchanged her old labels for new ones, who had experienced God plucking her from out of the pit.

Can you, too, sing of how your Redeemer has pursued your heart until it was His? Does your smile and song give evidence of your shiny new labels in Christ? Will your lips, too, shout for joy—you who have been redeemed?

Receiving His Redeeming Love

Think back upon God's grace and redeeming love in your life. What has He delivered you from?

Read the following verses. List the labels God places on you to tell your redemption story.

Psalm 30:4

    My new label:_____

John 15:15

    My new label:_____

2 Corinthians 5:17

    My new label:_____

1 Peter 2:9

    My new label:_____

1 John 3:1

    My new label:_____

Secular counseling, psychiatric therapy, and statistics tell us we will most likely repeat the patterns of our past or the patterns of those who influenced us most as we grew up. Yet if we're Christians, according to 1 Corinthians 5:17, we are set free from the old patterns of the past. Write that verse here, inserting your name into the verse and personalizing it. Then thank God for its truth in your life.

    🌹 🌹 🌹

A Prayer from the Heart

Thank You, God, that You are a redeeming God who pulled my life out of the pit. Thank You that I can be confident that You who began a good work in me will complete it (Philippians 1:6) and You will never give me up or let me go back to who I used to be. Thank You that so-called generational sin, bad habits, family tendencies, or statistics have no hold on me because I am new in You, and You possess the power to keep me and uphold me. Help me to wear with confidence the new labels You have given me—the labels of Friend, Beloved, Saint, Bride, One Whose Heart God Pursues.

A Gentle Blowing That Comforts and Consoles

I don't want to do this anymore, the old man must have thought as he lifted his heavy eyes toward heaven and pleaded with God to take his life.

He had lived harder in the last two days than most people do in a lifetime. And he was ready to call it quits. This man received bad reviews. People didn't appreciate him. In fact, a few people hated him. Yet all he had done was to try to serve the Lord. Could he have wondered if it was worth it anymore? In one day, this tired old man had climbed to the top of a mountain, challenged the political and religious systems of the day, prayed with all his might, seen God rain down fire from heaven and, in a surge of God-given anger, stabbed and killed 450 men who were enemies of the Almighty. And if that wasn't enough, his aged body ran 16 miles *in the rain,* only to discover, when he finally reached his destination, that he was on the queen's hit list and would need to run some more. So he continued running all night to another town, and in the morning he walked another day's distance into the desert.

Finally, he was alone. His muscles ached from exhaustion, his stomach longed for food, and his emotions cried out for relief. It had been days since he'd heard from the Lord—and days since He'd seen the awesome power from God atop the mountain. He needed something—*anything*—from God to assure him that his Maker was still around. But at this point it was easier to ask to die.

God heard the prayer of this tired old man. A gust of wind blew up around the old man's feet, but God didn't take the man's life in the whirlwind that day. Then the rock he was standing on began to shatter, but the man still stood standing. A stream of fire shot down from heaven and blazed all around him, but it never touched his cloak. The earth beneath his feet shook violently, but the earthquake did not topple him. The tired old man hid his face and waited for the worst. Then a cool, quiet breeze blew upon his face, and God Almighty whispered to Elijah in the sound of a gentle blowing.[20]

What did God whisper? Maybe it was those reassuring words, *I understand.* Or maybe God just whispered Elijah's name, reminding him that He was his Creator and He knew the intentions of his heart. Maybe God whispered His own name and it was enough for Elijah to know he had a Rock and Refuge. Whatever it was, the force of Irresistible Love in that gentle whisper gave Elijah the strength to continue on.

Like Elijah, we as women often reach the point where we cry out for relief. *I don't want to do this anymore,* we cry. *No one understands. No one's helping. No one appreciates me. No one cares.*

Wendy recalls such a time in her life. The pain that surrounded her personal life, her ministry, her marriage, and her spiritual life was more than she could bear. Her journal page from a cold day in April 2000 showed her stress, her weariness, and her readiness, like Elijah, to give up:

> *I'm hurting inside more than I thought. O Lord, bring healing, strength, rest! There are times I want healing and other times I just want to forget everything I know and be stubborn, curl up, and do nothing. My heart is breaking—no matter what anyone says to me, or does for me, I feel it's only because they "have to." I don't feel a genuine concern or love, I'm too unworthy. I'm tempted to just run away—get away—by myself. Life would go on, people would get along just fine...I'll just become apathetic towards life, Christianity, marriage, everything—going, doing what I must, yet dead inside.*

Where does a woman like Wendy go when she feels she's at the end of her rope? Who can get inside her heart and mind and figure things out when nothing else makes sense? Wendy went to her God in the only way she knew how. She asked for a way out, but God, instead, gave her a way through. She waited for His hammer to come down on her head. She, instead, felt the sweet softness of a gentle blowing.

Her gentle blowing was God's reminder that she was loved, through a husband who fought for her, through some close friends who didn't give up on her, through God's Word that spoke to the depths of her heart.

Wendy held onto the hope she had from Scripture—that God knows the plans He has for her, plans to not harm her, but to give her a future and a hope.[21] "I was holding out for that hope," she said.

Two and a half years later, Wendy's journal recorded the presence of a healing, gentle blowing in her life:

> *Lord, You are showing me so many things in my life that I'm filled with awe in what You are doing! Keep me close to You and to Your Word— I hunger for Your daily healing in my life. I want to be a godly example to others. I like how I've been feeling lately. I can once again be in a group of people and share and be myself and like it, instead of hiding off to the side or avoiding certain situations. I'm feeling more and more like myself again. Thank You, Lord, for the blessings You have given me! I will learn what disciplines are necessary to my prayer life, and I will faithfully practice them—without fail. Bless me, Lord, for I am Your servant.*

What brought Wendy from despair to determination to live for Him again? "There were so many situations and conflicts that brought me from one point to the next and God has taught me many things," she says. "But He mostly taught me about Himself! I don't know all the answers and I can't see why He did certain things, but I know God is good—all the time!"

God's Word says that when we are at our weakest, that's when He can be at His strongest, through us.

God pursued Wendy's heart through a gentle blowing that still breezes through her heart and mind, reminding her of His unfailing love.

My friend, the same God who ministered to Elijah— and to Wendy—can meet our cry, too, with gentleness and guidance, assuring us that we are not alone, that we have the Maker of the Universe and the Maker of our Soul on our side. And isn't that what we need at times? To know we are not alone? To know that the Almighty is on our side?

Like Elijah, we too can feel unstoppable at times. We can ride the tide in perfect form and conquer our opponents single-handedly. We go on and on and on with the rush of adrenalin, doing what must be done. But there eventually comes a time when our strength runs out, too, and we break under the pressure. We hear that one person has it out for us and we crumble to pieces, feeling broken and alone. And, like Elijah in his weakest moment, we're tired and ready to give up. Like Wendy, in the pit of despair, we cry out to the only one who can help us.

That's when this same God who met tired old Elijah in the sound of a gentle blowing can meet *us* and encourage us in the midst of our weakness. In fact, God stands waiting to calm our confusion and penetrate our pain with a peace that brings order to chaos and healing to open wounds.

God's Word says that when we are at our weakest, that's when He can be at His strongest, through us. In the Bible, the apostle Paul struggled with a matter he felt was too much for him. He asked God to relieve him of the burden, yet God's response was, "My gracious favor is all you need. My power works best in your weakness" (2 Corinthians 12:9 NLT). So feelings of defeat, exhaustion, fear, loneliness, inadequacy, and despair are invitations to rely on the strength of God which can soothe our present state and get us back to where we need to be.

Are *you* feeling defeated, emotionally exhausted, afraid and alone, ready to give up? Do *you* long to hear something—*anything*—from God, to know He is still for you, or that He is just there? The same God who can split the rocks and send down fire from heaven can also speak softly and tenderly to our hearts. And His message to us is this: "Come to Me; I know you're exhausted. Rest here awhile. Lay your load down on *My* shoulders and see how I will carry it for you. Get to know My gentleness, feel the warmth of My love, and experience peace and relief."[22] If you haven't felt that peace and relief for some time, maybe it's time to slow down and listen for the sound of God's gentle blowing. Maybe a second look at God's softer side will give you the strength you need to continue on and the courage you desire to come back to His arms.

Because God knows our weaknesses, our vulnerabilities, and our fears, He knows just how and when to communicate His tenderness toward us, like He did to Elijah. And often, if we get quiet enough to hear, we will sense when He calls us to drink of His stream that never runs dry, or walk along His path that will ever satisfy,[23] or feel Him in the breeze as He passes by.

The next time you feel as if you can't go on, remember your Source of strength and how it sometimes shows up in the gentlest breeze. And remember a promise in His Word: "Though the Lord gave you adversity...he will still be with you to teach you" (Isaiah 30:20 NLT). How? In the words that He whispers to you when you need direction (verse 21). In the way He speaks to you through His Word. In the peace that He gives you in the midst of your pain. In the gentle breeze on your face when you look toward heaven.

Would you like to hear His whisper the next time you feel alone? Do you long to feel His comforting presence instead of the pain? Would you like to be able to discern His voice, over your shoulder, telling you which way to walk?

You can. But first, stop waiting for the rocks to crack and the thunder to roll. Instead, be still and listen for the gentle voice of God. Pour out your heart to Him and wait for His comfort. Then you will discover His softer side—the side that communicates Irresistible Love. The side that once bled so you could be near Him. The side that listens to you, longs for you, and lifts you up through the sound of a gentle blowing.

Sensing His Gentle Blowing

What in your life is causing you to feel alone and discouraged?

In what ways do you need to sense the gentle blowing of God's relief?

How do you feel knowing that God responded to tired old Elijah in a cool, comforting breeze?

What does this tell you about the "God of all comfort" and how He stands ready to respond to you?

🌹   🌹   🌹

A Prayer from the Heart

Lord, I long for the sweet sound of a gentle blowing in my life. Please heal those open wounds of worry, fear, busyness, and anxiety in my life and bring me to a place of calm and stillness in my heart and mind where I can still hear Your voice. Thank You for knowing just how to reach me when my worries and fears carry me far from You. Thank You that your Word tells me that each day You carry me in Your arms.[24] Help me to trust and obey and to "take captive every thought to make it obedient to Christ" (2 Corinthians 10:5). O Lord, where would I be without Your calming, soothing, gentle blowing?

An Encouraging Friend Who Cheers You On

My then-four-year-old Dana was about to come on stage for her first dance recital. For the first hour of the program, I sat with my family, nervously fidgeting through the various performances. Now was the moment we'd been waiting for, and my stomach was tied up in knots!

What if she slips while walking onto the stage? What if she forgets the steps? What if she has stage fright and just stares at the audience? My mind thought of nearly everything that could go wrong. Finally, I got a grip on my panic mode and realized my only concern—and hope—was that she do her best and feel great about it.

She did. And after her performance, I sighed with relief. I had been her No. 1 Supporter in the audience, her No. 1 Fan, and her No. 1 Worrier.

Sometimes we think God has it out for us. We think He gives us opportunities and waits to see us fall. But He's the one who's cheering for us. Like a proud parent in the bleachers or a nervous mom in the recital hall, God wants to see us do our best and glorify Him. He is our No. 1 Encourager.

Encouragement is a lost art these days. It's hard to find. I have been fortunate enough to be surrounded by women in my church, or women I've met while out speaking whom I've stayed connected with, who have been a real source of encouragement to me. One of the encouragers in my life is Robin. Every time I talk with Robin she gets so excited to hear of my successes, my plans she's certain will be successes, and my discouragements that she's determined are predecessors to my successes. How I thrive on conversations with her! After talking on the phone with her, I feel reenergized and ready to conquer the world. My Aunt June is the same way. I've never had a conversation with her in which she hasn't rallied behind me and become my enthusiastic cheerleader.

That's the way God encourages us, like a devoted friend who wants to see us succeed. Psalm 20:4-5 says that He is, in a sense, our cheerleader on the sidelines, rooting for us and pushing us on toward victory: "May He grant your heart's desire, and fulfill all your plans," said David the psalmist. "May we *shout for joy when we hear of your victory*, flying banners to honor our God. May the LORD answer all your prayers" (NLT). In *The Message*, that verse reads: "When you win, we plan to raise the roof and lead the parade with our banners. May all your wishes come true!"

Imagine that. A banner set up for your victory. Imagine God, singing for joy over your victory, raising the roof in

> *In His gentle encouragement, He reminds us that it isn't what we do that pleases Him, it's who we are—His!*

celebration, like a proud parent rooting for His child's team on the field.

In Exodus 17, Moses set up a banner in the wilderness and called it Jehovah Nissi—the Lord is my banner. He is my victory. My Motivator. My Source of Strength. My Encourager.

The prophet Jeremiah tells us that the Lord knows the plans He has for us and those plans are not for our failure, but for our success, so that we can have a future and a hope (Jeremiah 29:11). God knows how important it is for us to have hope. We need things to look forward to. We need goals to strive for. We need a future. We need hope.

Knowing that He has already planned my future and my accomplishments gives me great confidence in whatever I set out to do. And if it's something that is in agreement with His will, that I'm doing with a sincere heart, and it is something that He sees is best for me, then I can be sure He is there to root me on—singing my victory song and setting up my banner.

If you can't hear God cheering for you or see Him out in the stands flying your banner, maybe it's because He's right behind you, whispering sweet words of encouragement and direction. Isaiah 30:21 says "Your ears will hear a voice behind you, saying, 'This is the way, walk in it.'" How wonderful to know God is there to navigate when the way gets confusing or the path is blocked.

Even God's ways of encouragement are encouraging. He knows when we need to hear shouts that will motivate us to drive on toward the finish line. And He knows when we would do better with a softly spoken word of encouragement that will gently push us forward. What I love most about Him, though, is that He also encourages us to slow down, take a rest, and not do some of the things the world tells us we must do in order to be "successful." In

His gentle encouragement, He reminds us that it isn't what we do that pleases Him, it's who we are—His!

I often tell my daughter, Dana, "I don't care whether or not you win, or whether or not you get the highest grade. I care only that you do your best and you enjoy doing it." Isn't that God's desire for us? To love Him with all our heart, soul, mind, and strength and to enjoy Him forever?

The things Dana has done for me that mean the most are not necessarily the things she's done perfectly, but the things she's done *from her heart*. When God sees His loved ones serving Him from their heart, He gladly steps up to lovingly encourage us.

Ruth Myers, in her book *The Perfect Love*, says,

> Our heavenly Father does not expect us to do everything perfectly. Even at our best we've still got our dirty thumbs in the glass. That's true in all our service. We'll serve Him perfectly in heaven, but never here. But God understands. He accepts imperfect service because it's a love relationship. He's a Father who's delighted that we love Him and want to please Him.[25]

God taught this to Sophie in a precious way. As a performer, she would often go into an audition thinking about how much better she could do than everyone else. She would then put a tremendous amount of pressure on herself to perform perfectly, both for herself and the auditor. In cases when she didn't get the job, she would be very hard on herself and even sink into depression. After sharing this with her pastor, Sophie was encouraged to take a different approach the next time she auditioned. Her pastor told her to glorify God with her talent by offering her audition as a gift to Jesus—not for the auditor or herself, but just for God.

Prior to Sophie's next audition—for a part she desperately wanted and needed—she hid in a bathroom stall and prayed, asking God to help her do her best *for Him*. When she walked onto the stage to face the auditors, who were by that time tired and ready to go home, she said her name and agency, spoke to the pianist, and stood in a marked spot to start the song.

Then, feeling a rush of warmth over her, she suddenly remembered that Jesus was right there in front of her. It was as if He had said, "Sophie, I got My ticket for the show; sing to Me!" She looked up and imagined Jesus sitting between the bored auditors with a great big smile, encouraging her.

That was all she needed.

"I sang my song and a voice from somewhere else sprang out of my throat and sure enough, I did beautifully—not for me, not for my auditors, but for Jesus!" Sophie recalls. What a difference it made for Sophie to focus on the one who was encouraging her rather than on her own abilities or imperfections.

Sophie's priorities changed that day. When she got a call-back from the auditors the next day, saying she did a fabulous job and they'd like to see her again, she realized that whether or not she got the part, she had been "the winner" in the eyes of her Lord. "I had already decided that I got the part that day because I knew it wasn't for me, but for Jesus."

What if every time you and I took a shot at something, we remembered that our No. 1 Fan was right there, smiling at us from the audience, rooting for us in the stands, encouraging us all the way? What a difference it would make, no matter how we performed.

Take heart, my friend. Your No. 1 Fan not only has your best in mind. He sees your heart, allowing you the confidence that, even in failure, if it's done for Him, it's a success.

So press on. And listen for the applause from heaven. Whether it's shouts in the stadium, smiles in the audience, or whispers during your weakest moments, are *you* listening for the tender words and looking for the sweet smile of *His* encouragement?

Responding to His Whispers

Philippians 4:13 says "I can do everything through him who gives me strength." In what ways has He strengthened you to accomplish your dreams and goals?

Do you have any dreams or goals that are interfering with your relationship with God? If so, they need to be redirected. Ask God to show you which goals are pleasing in His sight and attainable through Him.

What kinds of encouraging whispers have you heard lately?

Sometimes God's encouragement comes from people He puts in our path, sometimes from verses of Scripture we read. If you're not sure, ask God to help you recognize when He is encouraging you and nudging you forward. (For more on hearing God's voice, see chapter 9, "Listening to His Loving Voice" in *Letting God Meet Your Emotional Needs* by Cindi McMenamin, Harvest House Publishers, 2003.)

❧   ❧   ❧

A Prayer from the Heart

Thank You, Jesus, for being my No. 1 Fan. It's good to know that, like a parent, You want my best...and You truly want me to succeed, but only if it's for my own good and Your glory. Please open my eyes to see Your gentle ways of encouraging me—just when I need it most, just when I feel there's no one else to come behind me. And keep whispering in my ear, "This is the way...walk in it!" This time, I will listen.

Your Loyal Lover Who Will Never Leave

I remember the first time I fell in love. I was 18. So was he. He was handsome, charming, and the one I believed I would marry. But, about a year after our relationship began, it seemed to end. Several times. Each time the love of my life broke up with me—so that he could see if he really loved me or if we really were meant to be together—I found that he seemed to love me even more when he returned. It appeared, many times, that our "time away" from each other helped our relationship improve, at least for a while. Then the day came that he backed out of my life for good.

Shortly after, I met Hugh. Just as things were going really well in our long-distance relationship, I prepared myself for the worst.

"Hugh, if ever you need some time away, so that our relationship can be better, just let me know," I told him one evening as he was getting ready to drive the four hours back to his college campus. It was then that Hugh informed me that he wasn't the type of man who would ever ask for time away.

"Why?" I asked, thinking he wasn't willing to invest in the relationship.

"*God* never wants time away from you, Cindi," he told me, as he looked directly in my eyes. "So neither will I."

When Hugh said that, he not only opened my eyes to the fact that I had found a man who intended to love me as God does, but that I had a Lover, all along, who never wanted time away from me. I truly had a love, in the Lord Jesus, who would never leave me.

In Hebrews 13:5, we are told that God will never leave us or desert us. And in Psalm 139, we learn that not only will He never leave us, but He'll never let us out of His sight.

> "Where can I go from Your Spirit?" David, the psalmist, asks God. "Where can I flee from Your presence? If I go up to the heavens (*or, if I'm on top of the world and everything is fine and I don't need you*), you are there; if I make my bed in the depths (*or, sink so low in my depression or despair that no one else wants to be around me*), you are there; If I rise on the wings of the dawn (*or, pack up and move out*) if I settle on the far side of the sea (*if I wall myself into a cave where no one can hurt me again*), even there your hand will guide me, Your right hand will hold me fast. If I say 'Surely the darkness will hide me and the light become night around me (*certainly, because of the sin in my life, you'll want nothing to do with me*),' even the darkness will not be dark to You..." (verses 7-12, my paraphrase in italics).

What a love story! No matter where we go or what happens to us, God is there. He not only will never leave us, but He'll never let us out of His sight. He will stick to us like glue. We can't lose Him, even if we try.

Now where on earth can we find a love like that?

Most of us believe we find it when we find "the perfect man."

Shirley believed she had found a lover who would never leave. She and Ed had been happily married for 24 years. When Ed was offered a newly developed surgery to help him with weight control and to lessen his chances of a heart attack later in life, he and Shirley were excited about it, believing they were being given an opportunity for a longer life together, which would include enjoying grandchildren and traveling to several places they had always wanted to see. The surgery went well, but on the last day of recovery, just before Ed could pack up to go home, an unexpected infection set in and took his life.

"All that would come out of my mouth was *no!*" Shirley recalls after getting the devastating news. "I remember feeling completely stunned, the room seemed to be spinning around me. Christi (her nine-year-old daughter) clung to me and there was almost a sensation of drowning."

Do you long for a Lover who will never leave? You have one, in the God who pursues your heart.

Then, just as if loving arms encircled her, Shirley remembers being aware of God's presence in the most profound way. She calls it an expression of His love for her that left her speechless.

"The feeling of His being right there beside me, holding me in His arms could not have been more real.

Because of God's great love given to us at that time, Christi and I were able to go forward in our lives knowing by experience that God never leaves us or forsakes us and that He is indeed able to be, and truly is, a husband to the widow and a father to the fatherless.[26] I can't imagine what our lives would have been like without our loving Lord."

Although Shirley at one time never imagined that her husband would leave, she now realizes that no matter what happens here on earth or beyond the grave, she'll never have to endure the loss of a husband again. Not only has she chosen not to remarry, but she is enjoying life with her heavenly Husband, Jesus, who will never leave, and anticipating the day she will be reunited with Ed.

Carole has also learned the beauty of a Lover who will never leave. While I was speaking at her church's retreat a few years ago, she came up to me afterward and shared about her divorce and remarriage after her first husband left her for another woman.

"I used to be really sad that my second husband doesn't share with me my history, he doesn't share all the memories of when my kids were growing up, like my first husband does. I used to feel sad that I was alone in that. But after considering that God is my spiritual husband, I realized that I do have a Husband who knows my history and has lived it with me."

Carole is precious in God's sight. And she now knows she has a Husband who has never left and never will.

Do you long for a Lover who will never leave? You have one, in the God who pursues your heart. To the highest mountain, to the lowest part of the sea, He will not let you out of His sight. That is a powerful pursuing love. And that's the love He has for you.

It's possible you've known lovers who have left. It's possible that every man you've ever trusted has betrayed you. But one Man stands apart from the rest. "Greater love has no one than this," Jesus said, "that he lay down his life for his friends" (John 15:13). And then Jesus did just that. He Himself demonstrated "greater love"—the greatest love—by laying down His life for you and me.

Now if not even the grave could keep Him away from us, then nothing can! His love has true staying power. So, won't you let Him be *your* Lover Who Never Leaves?

Relying on His Ever-Present Love

Fill in the blanks to write a personal song (much like Psalm 139:7-12) that tells others of the places you have gone where the Lord has followed:

> Where can I go from your Spirit, Lord? How can I lose You? If I _____,
> You are there. If I run to _____,
> behold, You are there. If I pack up and move
> out to _____, still You
> are with me; if I say _____,
> You will still pursue my heart and not let me
> out of Your sight.

Now, write a brief thank you to your loyal Lover Who Never Leaves:

🌿 🌿 🌿

A Prayer from the Heart

Lord, You have searched me and known me. You know all about what I long for in love and life. Thank You that You are the epitome of what I want and need in a love that will never leave. Remind me, when I start to wander, that there's nowhere I can go where Your love will not follow me and find me and pursue me back into Your arms. May I, too, be called *Your* lover who never leaves.

A Proud Father Who Clothes You in White

I remember the excitement—and frustration—of shopping for the perfect wedding dress. It had to be fluffy, with lots of sequins...a real Cinderella gown. After all, I was marrying my prince and everything needed to be just right. After weeks of trying on dress after dress, I finally found it. When I first saw it glistening in the window of a small bridal shop in my hometown, my heart leaped. *That's it!* I thought. *That's my dress!* But my heart sunk when I saw the price tag. At that time, $550 was a lot of money to come up with for a dress to wear on one day of my life, even though it would be the most special day of my life.

I went home and waited for the right time to approach my Dad. Dad had been paying my college tuition for four years and was helping me with the rent on my apartment as well. He had already put money down for a wedding cake, flowers, and photographs. I feared the cost of my dress might send him over the edge!

When I peeked around the door of my Dad's bedroom, where he was resting in front of the television after a long day of work, I hesitantly told him that I found my dream dress. When I told him how much it cost, I could tell he was concerned. After a moment of silence, Dad simply said, like he has so many times throughout my life, "I'll find a way, Ceenee...you go get your dress."

There was a sense of pride and warmth in me as I went back to the shop and said, "I'll take it." I knew I hadn't made the purchase possible; my Dad had. But the overwhelming feeling of being loved and cared for added to the special gift he gave me that day. I assume my Dad has long since forgotten the price of that dress and what he had to give up so that I could be dressed in that particular white dress. But the sacrifice on his part, and the willingness for him to "find a way" to provide for his daughter, has stayed with me all these years. Today, that story gives me a glimpse of what my heavenly Father paid centuries ago to clothe me in white for an even more special day.

Of all the things we want in life...there is only one thing we truly need: the righteousness of God.

God's Word says in Isaiah 61:10, "I delight greatly in the LORD; my soul rejoices in my God. For he has clothed me with garments of salvation and arrayed me in a robe of righteousness, as a bridegroom adorns his head like a priest, as a bride adorns herself with her jewels."

Have you considered what it cost God our Father 2,000 years ago to clothe us in righteousness—to make us spotless and white for that special day when we stand before Him? It cost Him a lot more than $550. It cost Him the life and blood of His precious Son, Jesus, on a hill called Calvary. God wasn't happy about the cost, but He knew it had to be done. And He found a way—The Way, the Truth and the Life[27] in the person of Jesus.

We can now echo Isaiah's proclamation: "I delight greatly in the LORD; my soul rejoices in my God. For he clothed me with garments of salvation and arrayed me in a robe of righteousness...."

Of all the things we want in life—a beautiful wedding day, a love that lasts, memories that are priceless—there is only one thing we truly need: the righteousness of God. Our Father in heaven knew that—so much so that He found a way, regardless of the price, to provide that for us.

God told His people in Isaiah 1:18: "Come now, let us reason together.... Though your sins are like scarlet, they shall be as white as snow; though they are red as crimson, they shall be like wool." He wants to reason with us, as well, and convince us that our greatest need is Him and His holiness and that when we seek Him first, all the other things we need will fall into place.[28]

Is it time for you to reason with Him? Is it time you see that your greatest need is not to live happily ever after or have a husband or be fulfilled in love, but to have His holiness and righteousness credited to you and be dressed in a white robe for Him?

There have been many times in my life when I've slipped into the mode of believing I need God for all that He does for me...giving me peace, providing emotional fulfillment, being a husband to me, helping me parent my child, steering me in the right direction. But those are all added benefits to being in a relationship with God. The reality of my situation—and yours—is that I need God because I am unrighteous on my own...because I can never hit the mark of absolute holiness and perfection, which a holy and perfect God requires. If I didn't truly need His righteousness, His perfect, sinless Son Jesus would not have needed to die for me. Upon realizing that, I have often had to return to the grace of God and repent for coming to Him for what I need rather than coming to Him simply because He is God and He is worthy of my surrender and praise.

Because He has pursued my heart relentlessly by providing, through His Son's death, a garment of white for me, I can wear my robe with dignity and with the assurance that I am much loved.

What about you? What will *your* dress look like on the day when you stand before God? Will it be spotless and white? It can be. Go to your Father in heaven, acknowledge your need to be wrapped in His righteousness and stand amazed as He shows you the cost—the nail prints in the hands of His precious Son—and then wraps you in white.

Reflecting on His Righteousness

Think about all the preparations that are made for a wedding. Now consider that Jesus has been making those preparations for you since He left this earth. Reflect on that for a moment as you consider how important that "wedding day" is to Him.

Can you recall times in your life when you relied on your own good intentions and acts of kindness to please God? Yet His Word clearly says, "There is no one righteous, not even one" (Romans 3:10). Take a few moments to write out your gratitude to God for doing what was necessary to clothe you in righteousness:

A Prayer from the Heart

What a wonderful Father You are, Lord God! From the moment I needed to be clean, You made plans to do what was necessary to clothe me in white. May I always wear the robes of Your righteousness with dignity, remembering that I represent You in all I say and do. Help me to hold my head high as the much-loved daughter of the King. For You alone, and because of You alone, I can be white as snow.

A Bridegroom Who Promises to Return

I'll never forget the evening Hugh asked me to marry him. It was the most wonderful night of my life. And yet there was sadness. It was a wonderful night because of the hope that we shared, for the first time, that we would one day never have to be apart again. But it was sad because the following morning he would head back to Bible school and we'd be, once again, separated by 200 miles. The morning after Hugh asked me to marry him, he got in his car and drove back to Southern California, where he was finishing his first year of college. But before leaving, he handed me a card. In that card, I found the heart of a man who was relating to Christ and His commitment to come for us, the church, and one day be with us forever.

Never before had I realized the parallel of our engagements here on earth to that of God, as our Beloved Bridegroom, and the anticipation He has in waiting for us to be completely His.

Hugh's card to me said this:

Tonight is a very special night. I have discovered that our situation of living apart in two different areas of the state has afforded me a rare opportunity to imitate my Lord. Some two thousand years ago, Christ did the same with us. He entered this world by traveling a great distance in order to seek out a bride to whom He could betroth Himself. Having found her, the church, He remained with her for a time and firmly established the engagement, giving her the signifying seal of the Holy Spirit to sanctify her. He soon departed and returned to where He had come from, but not without leaving His chosen bride-to-be a great promise: the promise of His ultimate return when He and His bride would be permanently united, accompanied by a grand marriage feast. From that moment on, they would be one, inseparable by time or distance—they would be one.

I have made a journey, Cindi, of some 200 miles in order to come to a woman who I desire to be my wife…having searched for her and knowing where she is, I have gently requested her engagement, giving to her a precious symbol, a seal, that would set her apart for her groom. That is the ring. Although I must leave after a time and return home, there remains in the mind of the bride a promise of hope: I will return and on the occasion of my returning there will be a most beautiful wedding.…"

Because we are promised to Him, the rest of our lives here on earth should be lived in joyful preparation for the wedding.

I remember the ache I felt in my heart as Hugh drove away that morning...and during the four long months before our wedding date would bring us together. Yet how much *longer* our Lord has waited for us, His bride, so that we, too, can be inseparable!

Have you considered the love story of His engagement to you? At salvation, we were engaged to Christ. He placed His Holy Spirit in us as a pledge,[29] much like a bridegroom places a ring on the finger of his bride-to-be. Because we are promised to Him, the rest of our lives here on earth should be lived in joyful preparation for the wedding. We announce to everyone around that we are in love and will soon be with the One whom we love. We plan and prepare and do things that will please Him upon His return. We arrange for our spotless, white dress for that special day, we invite family and friends to join us in the celebration, we go out of our way to make everything perfect for the time that our Bridegroom will return.

But the preparation carries with it a longing as well that is downright painful at times. Like Hugh, who had to drive away right after the engagement, our Bridegroom had to depart to prepare a place where we will live with Him forever. Naturally, all we can think about while He is gone is our longing for His return so we can be together face to face. Our hearts ache for Him.

In her book *Taking Up Your Cross,* author Tricia McCary Rhodes writes:

> Everyday He comes to us, every minute He continues to woo us, calling us with amorous overtures...thoughts of Him pervade all that we do. We cry out, "hurry my beloved, and be like a gazelle or a young stag on the mountain of spices" (Song of Solomon 8:14). Living in a

love affair with our Lord and believing His promise to come again compels us to keep ourselves clothed and ready for Him....Nothing He asks of us is too hard—His commands are not burdensome for love motivates all we do.[30]

Do you live with a longing for your Bridegroom? Is your love for Him motivating all you do? Maybe you sense a longing for His work rather than just for Him. Perhaps you long for His justice to make this world right. Maybe you long for His completed work in your life so you will no longer sin. Maybe you long for the gathering of His church so all Christians will experience unity at last. Maybe you long to see a loved one who is already with Him. There are many reasons we might long for Christ's return. But do you long for just Him—Him alone?

The letter Jesus left us at our engagement speaks of *His* longing to simply be with us—as a new husband longs to start his new life with his wife: "Do not let your hearts be troubled. Trust in God; trust also in me. In my Father's house are many rooms.... I am going there to prepare a place for you. And...I will come back and take you to be with me that you also may be where I am" (John 14:1-4).

God's pursuing love counts the days until we will be together for the wedding feast. Are *you* counting the days as well?

Preparing for the Bridegroom

What will be the most exciting aspect of being with Christ, your Bridegroom, face to face?

In what ways can you prepare now for His imminent return?

Jesus left you a love letter (the Bible), recording His longings to be with you. Would you write Him a few lines telling Him how you long to be with Him as well?

❧   ❧   ❧

A Prayer from the Heart

Lord, sow in me a longing for You so that my heart's cry is, "Come quickly, Lord Jesus, and take me home with You." Don't let my eyes stray from You, but keep me focused on You, my Bridegroom, and the perfect life we will one day share together. From this day forward, may I only have eyes—and a heart—for You.

Your Hero Who Always Comes Through

eidre recalls the evening she sat in her chair in her apartment, praying because she didn't have any money to pay her rent. A series of circumstances beyond her control left her penniless that month. Five o'clock was an hour away and if she did not have the money in her landlord's office by then, she would be evicted the following morning. As she was praying, calling out to God as the Scriptures tell us to do, the phone rang. It was someone at Deidre's church, offering to pay the rent. Just in the knick of time, Deidre's Hero had come through.

Do you know what it's like to get that unexpected check in the mail on Monday, which gives you enough money to pay for that unexpected car repair that hits you on Tuesday? Do you ever find that the phone call to encourage you comes just at the right moment or a letter you received three days earlier is opened on the exact day that you needed to read it? So-called "coincidences" like these convince me that we have a Hero in the wings, working to help you and me. Whether it's through a timely word of encouragement from a friend, a healing phone call at the moment of crisis, or a verse of Scripture that jumps off the page and speaks to your heart for the situation at hand, our God is One who, in His perfect timing, always comes through.

My friend recently lost her job. But a day before it happened, she got a letter from an employment agency inquiring about her availability. She disregarded it the day she got it. But the next day, that letter represented to her a gentle reminder from God, as if He were saying: "I know all about it, My child, and I'm already working on Your behalf."

Each time a publisher rejected the manuscript for my first book, there was something else that arrived in the mail just in time before I lost hope. Now that, to me, represents a God who arranges the chess pieces in our lives and works out the details constantly so we have just what we need just when we need it. Again, I call that the work of a Hero...a God who loves to come through.

I see that kind of God in Scripture time and time again. I see a God who, when the odds are stacked up, at the precise moment of great need, comes valiantly to the rescue of His people.

Remember the Israelites? Trapped between the Egyptian army and the Red Sea? God waited until the Israelites could feel the rumble of horses' hooves under their feet and feel the mist from the sea on their backs before He parted those waters and let His people walk through on dry land. Then He finished the job, closing the waters—right after every Israelite made it through—and catching the "bad guys" just in the nick of time. How He must have loved the awe that His people felt as they sang and danced for their Hero who came through for them.[31]

When the Israelites prepared to battle the Midianites, God told their leader, Gideon, "You have too many men for me to deliver Midian into your hands." God told Gideon He wouldn't let Israel have the victory if there was any chance they'd boast of their own strength. He wanted it very apparent that it was He who won their battles. So God told Gideon to tell the people that whoever was timid or afraid could leave—and 22,000 soldiers dropped out! And God's response? "There are *still* too many men." God pared down Gideon's army to only 300 men, who ended up defeating an army of 15,000 Midianites by blowing on horns, breaking jars, and yelling, "A sword for the Lord and for Gideon." Now, that is a battle that could only be planned, executed, and won by a God who loves to come through![32]

Why do you think women like you and I, in the depths of our heart, long for a hero? Why do we love romance novels in which a hero comes through for the girl just in the nick of time? Why do our hearts skip a beat when we see a man in the movies risk it all to save his woman? I believe God made us with hearts to resonate in response to the kind of God that He is—a Hero who always comes through.

Several years ago, I worked as a reporter for a seaside newspaper bureau. There were evenings when the job called for staying late at meetings and calling in the results of the meeting to a night copy editor at the main newspaper office in order to get the story in the next morning's paper. That late-night deadline situation often led to stressed-out copy editors at the main office, and there was one who was particularly nasty, often leaving the female reporters on the other end of the phone in tears.

On one particular night, I was sitting at a city council meeting, completely unaware that Mr. Nasty was the night editor that evening and was going berserk back at the main office about my meeting results that had not yet been called in. The editor called Andy, the senior reporter in my bureau, complaining that I had not yet checked in. Andy sensed that the night editor was about ready to lose it and, knowing it would be my first phone encounter with Mr. Nasty, he wanted to shield me from that. Andy left his home about 10:30 P.M. and drove 20 minutes to the council meeting, whispered a question to me about status, and then left the room quietly to make "the comfort call" to the cranky editor. He then offered to stay and make the final call for me so that I could get on the road earlier for my long drive home. I didn't find out that Andy had intercepted the angry editor for me until the next morning, when the buzz around the newsroom was about "what Andy did last night for another one of the bureau girls."

No man will ever be able to come through for us like Jesus did.

That whole day, I couldn't get out of my mind what this guy had done for *me*. (After that incident, Andy was nicknamed "the women's white knight." But let me tell you, there wasn't a woman in that place who didn't think Andy was THE MAN after that.)

You and I have a Man who not only constantly monitors our situation and steps in when we need encouragement or relief, but who—through His death for us on Calvary—became God's greatest provision for us, His greatest gift for us, His greatest demonstration of His love for us.

No man will ever be able to come through for us like Jesus did.

But what about those times when it appears as if God will not come through? We can all recall times when we wondered if God really was working on our behalf.

In Psalm 77, we read about Asaph looking at his situation and feeling as if God had abandoned him. He cried out to God, asking, "Will the Lord reject forever? Will he never show his favor again? Has his unfailing love vanished forever? Has his promise failed for all time? Has God forgotten to be merciful? Has he in anger withheld his compassion?" (verses 7-10).

Apparently Asaph was worried that God would not come through. (And yet that is so like us to begin to worry when our circumstances look bad.) Then Asaph said, "I will remember the deeds of the LORD; yes, I will remember your miracles of long ago. I will meditate on all your works and consider all your mighty deeds" (verses 11-12).

When Asaph's heart started fearing that God was not there, his head told him what he knew to be true of God—that He's come through in the past, and He will come through again! Later in the psalm, Asaph makes a wonderful proclamation: "Your path led through the sea, your way through the mighty waters, though your footprints were not seen" (verse 19). In other words, God's method of coming through was not one Asaph would have guessed—and there wasn't a sign of God's presence (such as footprints or voices or a warm fuzzy feeling), even though He was definitely there. How often God rushes in to rescue us, leaving no sign that He was really there. Oftentimes it's not until later that we realize heaven came to earth to bail us out!

Do you need a hero in your life, your marriage, your job situation? God sometimes gives no indication of *how* He will help, but He always most definitely comes through. Start watching how He comes through for you.

Holding onto
Our Hero

Describe a time when God "came through" for you in the nick of time:

Read the following verses and write them here so you will have a record of God's strength and dependability when you need to rely on Him (you never know when you're going to need to look back and remember that you have a Hero working on your behalf):

Exodus 14:14—

Psalm 57:2—

Isaiah 43:2—

Isaiah 43:19—

❧   ❧   ❧

A Prayer from the Heart

Lord, You are the Hero who holds my heart, who comes through for me in the nick of time, who never lets me down. Thank You that as mighty and wonderful as You are, You still care about the intimate details of my life. When I start to worry that You won't come through, gently remind me of Your path that leads through the sea and Your mighty footprints that aren't always seen. Help me hold on to You.

Your White Knight Who Rushes to Your Rescue

*M*arie recalls the day danger almost envolped her.

She had intended to walk quickly past the gray van that was parked alongside the street on the way to her bus stop. But the man in the van got her attention when he sounded desperate. "Excuse me, I'm not from around here and I'm lost. Could you help me?" He appeared to be pointing to a map. Marie started to walk toward the van. The man looked friendly, she thought. But the closer she got, the more she hesitated. The man was by himself. The vans windows were tinted (and a bad tint job, too). She then saw that the "map" he was holding was actually a magazine. Fear pulsed through Marie's body as if everything within her said *run*. She turned on her heels, stammered, "No, I'm sorry, I can't help you" and began to walk quickly away from the van. She heard the van following behind her and the driver cursing at her, telling her to come back. When she looked back, the driver accelerated then braked through a puddle of water, spraying Marie and causing her to drop all her bags. She then heard a horn beeping and the driver of a red pickup truck yelled to the van driver, "Are you crazy, man?" The driver of the truck stopped, asked if Marie was okay, and then drove off after the gray van, which by then had sped away.

Marie grabbed her cell phone, called 9-1-1, and described the van and its driver, explaining what had happened. By then she was crying and apologizing for being so distraught. The operator assured Marie she had done the right thing. There had been a number of reports recently on the same van in the same area over the past few days, and the police had been working to track down the suspect.

❧   ❧   ❧

Deidre looked danger in the face as well. Her situation was not a man in a van, but a gun barrel pointed directly at her head. She and a friend were being mugged in Marina del Rey in California.

"In Jesus' name, let us go," Deidre called out, and the gunman was thrown backward, turned to run, turned back for a moment, and then shot the gun at Deidre's face. The shot completely missed her. After calling the police to the scene and explaining what had happened, Deidre and her friend were released unharmed and the police found the muggers within the hour.

❧   ❧   ❧

Sonya's danger occurred inside her body, and it almost took her life. She knew that the pain and bleeding she was experiencing had to be more than a miscarriage. When she began having heart palpitations, buzzing in her ears, tingling in her arms, and severe lightheadedness, she was rushed to the hospital, where doctors discovered a tremendous amount of blood loss. Sonya's fallopian tube had ruptured due to an ectopic pregnancy. It wasn't until the next morning, when Sonya was told that her right ovary had been removed, that she realized she had come within moments of death. She was also told that it was a good thing the pain medication she was prescribed for a misdiagnosed miscarriage made her sick. If she had kept the medication down, it would have make her sleepy and she could have bled to death had she not awakened to notice her bizarre symptoms.

What goes on in the heavenly realm when God's loved ones are in danger? Did God give Marie the overwhelming urge to run from the man in the gray van? Did the unseen heavenly forces rush to Deidre's help when that gun was pointed at her head? Did a signal sound in the skies when Sonya was approaching death?

I choose to believe so. That's the kind of rescuing God we have—One who "rides the skies" to come down and protect His own.[33] In the last chapter we looked at subtle ways that God comes through as our hero for the everyday details of our life. But what happens in the heavenly realm when God's beloved needs a full-fledged rescue?

In Psalm 18, David—a man who experienced many dramatic rescues by God—describes the scene that took place in heaven when he cried out to God for help and was delivered from a band of men trying to kill him. David says cords of death surrounded him, floods of destruction swept over him, and the grave wrapped its ropes around him. Death was staring him in the face (Psalm 18:4-5 NLT). David was obviously in a life-threatening situation. Now look at what happened when the cry reached God's ears, and imagine the scene on a big screen in full Technicolor and stereo surround sound:

> The earth trembled and quaked, and the foundations of the mountains shook; they trembled because he was angry. Smoke rose from his nostrils; consuming fire came from his mouth, burning coals blazed out of it. He parted the heavens and came down; dark clouds were under his feet. He mounted the cherubim and flew; he soared on the wings of the wind. He made darkness his covering, his canopy around him—the dark rain clouds of the sky. Out of the brightness of his presence clouds advanced, with hailstones and bolts of lightning. The LORD thundered from heaven; the voice of the Most High resounded. He shot his arrows and scattered the enemies, great bolts of lightning and routed them. The valleys of the sea were exposed and the foundations of the earth laid bare at your rebuke, O LORD, at the blast of breath from your nostrils (Psalm 18:7-15 NIV).

As with a climactic rescue scene in a movie, you can almost hear the thundering music in the background as God's strength and might is displayed. Then, imagine the music softening into a sweet melody that backdrops the tenderness of what happens next:

He reached down from on high and took hold of me; he drew me out of deep waters. He rescued me from my powerful enemy...He brought me out into a spacious place; he rescued me because he delighted in me (verses 16-17,19 NLT).

Now *that's* a rescue.

Can you imagine that scene taking place when *you* are in a threatening situation? Have you ever thought about God's flaring nostrils when someone messes with *you?* Can you picture His canopy of darkness that shoots down after someone wrongfully brings trouble upon you?

Perhaps not. Maybe this knightly rescue is difficult for you to imagine or believe. Perhaps you can recall times in your life, or in someone else's life, when it appeared God did not respond. What about the man in the van who got away? Or the gunshot that actually takes a woman's life? What about the surgery that goes wrong or the cancer that goes undetected? What does *that* say about a God who rescues?

When David wrote Psalm 18, I don't believe he actually saw what he described. He figuratively described it for us based on what he knew to be true about God. He wrote from a heart inspired by God to portray the imagery for you and me. And although you and I have not literally seen heaven open and God come rushing to our rescue, that doesn't mean God is silently and passively standing by when we encounter trouble.

When Job experienced his storm of endless trials and physical assaults, his friends all thought God had abandoned him. Even Job had no clue about the showdown that was occurring in heaven between God and Satan. So, too, you and I often have no idea of what is going on in the spiritual realm when our lives are threatened. But our trust in God tells us that He is good, and that sometimes He intervenes and thwarts the danger, and that sometimes He takes us home. But whatever He decides, it is good and perfect and just.

Job wasn't the only one who experienced attack here on earth, and later may have found out God had specifically ordered his life spared. The Israelites, even after they saw God rescue them by leading them through the Red Sea, still thought many times that God would not show up or come through on their behalf. Yet He always did.

I wonder if Mary was worried the night she was to give birth to Jesus. Wasn't God going before them? Didn't He know the exact timing of when His Son would be born? Why, then, was there no room at the inn? God was looking at a bigger picture, at the paradox of the King of Glory being born in a barn. At the prophecy that was to be fulfilled. At humbling Himself in every way so that He could relate to us even in the worst of our circumstances.

Mary may have had no thought of God as her Rescuer in what we think of as a "silent night." But in Revelation 12 we read that an all-out war occurred in heaven over the birth of Jesus as God's power crashed through the atmosphere so He could dwell among men on earth. God *was* fighting a battle in the heavenly realm as Jesus lay, seemingly unnoticed, in a cow's trough in a damp and smelly barn.

We may not always see it, but God is at work in the heavenly realm and... get this... He's at work on our behalf.

In 2 Kings 6, Elisha's servant was fearful when he saw that the king of Aram and his soldiers, with all their chariots and horses, had surrounded the city to take Elisha and his men by force. But Elisha's response was, "Don't be afraid.... Those who are with us are more than those who are with them." Then Elisha prayed that God would open the eyes of his servant so he could see the heavenly rescue in place on their behalf. Sure enough, "the LORD opened the servant's eyes, and he looked and saw the hills full of horses and chariots of fire all around Elisha."[34] Even though Elisha's servant couldn't originally see the heavenly army with his bare eyes, the army was in place and prepared!

And, when Jesus hung on the cross, it looked to the world like a defeat. He even cried the words, "My God, my God, why have you forsaken me?" (Matthew 27:46). But God had not forsaken or forgotten His beloved Son. God was working out the most incredible rescue in the history of mankind. And at the moment of Jesus' death, the thick and heavy veil in the temple in Jerusalem, which separated God from His people, was split into two from the top down.[35] The separation between God and man was over. Jesus had done it. The most wonderful, the most complete, the most daring rescue of all took place...and an earthquake and darkness across the land accompanied it. It was such an incredible rescue that a Roman guard who took part in the execution of Jesus profoundly said, "Surely this man was the Son of God!" (Mark 15:39).

We may not always see it, but God is at work in the heavenly realm and...get this...He's at work on *our* behalf. At the times when we think nothing is going on, we can be assured that the God of the heavens, who promises to work all things together for the good of those who love Him (Romans 8:28), is planning our rescue and relief. In Psalm 68:28, David remembers God's defense and deliverance and says: "Summon your power, O God; show us your strength, O God, as you have done before."

God has shown His strength many times before, and He will show it again. I often recall the story of what God our Defender did when a Middle Eastern king took Sarah, the wife of Abraham, and intended to make her his wife. The story makes the hair on my arms stand straight up! God didn't just take this in stride. He didn't overlook the crime. He showed His strength. God Almighty appeared to the king in a dream and sternly warned, in essence, "You're as good as dead if you don't give her back!" (Genesis 20:1-6.)

When someone messes with a woman after God's heart, there is literally hell to pay. That's the kind of love and protection that surrounds us when we are in relationship with our White Knight. But just in case the doubts rush in now and then, and you don't feel that you really have a knight, let me tell you what happened when I doubted that, too.

Just as I was writing this chapter, asking God for the words to express His heart to His beloved, the doubts raced in and I prayed, "Are you really a knight, God, or am I making this up? Do you really rescue with all the force and might and strength that a woman longs for? If so, God, show me that in Your Word. Show me where I can find a picture of You as a mighty rescuing knight." (I couldn't exactly look up "knight" in my concordance and get a barrage of verses!)

And God, the Faithful One, showed His strength once again.

In my reading that morning, I looked up Psalm 18, that wonderful description of God's rescue of David, in a different translation. To my surprise, the psalm opened with these breathtaking words: "I love you, GOD—you make me strong. GOD is bedrock under my feet, the castle in which I live, my *rescuing knight.*"[36]

There it is, tender heart. Take confidence in the fact that you *do* have a rescuing knight. And anyone who wants to mess with you has to go through God Almighty first.

Recalling a Knight's Tale

Can you recall a time when God rushed to your rescue? With Psalm 18 as a model, describe the scene here.

Look up the following verses. Write a few words about how God rescues you with all the strength and valor of a white knight.

Psalm 31:2—

Psalm 57:1—

Psalm 68:20—

Psalm 68:28—

Psalm 91:14-15—

Jeremiah 1:8—

Psalm 119:170 (NLT) says "Listen to my prayer; rescue me as you promised." Do you have a prayer, a sentence, a verse or a code word to immediately acknowledge your Valiant Knight's promise to rescue you? Write it here and tell Him about it. (He already knows, but He loves to hear of your confidence in Him.)

❧   ❧   ❧

A Prayer from the Heart

God, You truly are Bedrock under my feet, the safe and beautiful Castle in which I live, my Rescuing Knight. Thank you for the ways You rescue me in the little things and the wonderful way You rescued me from the biggest thing— the penalty of my sin. You truly are a God of Valor, Strength, and Deliverance. I want to live the rest of my life in loving gratitude for the ways You have rescued me. Thank You, dear Lord, for not stopping until You had won my heart.

Your Refuge Who Offers True Rest

I had been a whirlwind month for me. I'd been speaking every weekend and was trying to run a church women's ministry at the same time. And I was exhausted. I had gone away to a weekend retreat with my church women, but could stay only a day because I had to catch a 5:00 A.M. flight the next morning for a three-city media tour for interviews about my newest book.

I never took the time at the retreat to really relax, but apparently God was not going to have that! As I sat down on a Saturday morning, just hours before I'd leave to go home and pack up again for my next trip, I read this from Isaiah 28:12: "This is the resting place, let the weary rest." Something pulled at my heart at that moment.

Yeah, that would be nice…a resting place, I thought. But then I closed my Bible and started to walk away. *Wait,* I thought. *Where is the resting place? Here? At this retreat center in the mountains? Where, God? Because I have to leave in a little while anyway!* But His words would not leave my mind.

This is the resting place.

Suddenly I got it. This was the point at which I was to slow down and live sanely again. This was where it stopped. This was where God intervened and said, "Enough!" Something happened in my heart that day as I realized that my running to and fro was doing nothing but making me more tired. Was God capable of running the ministry He had entrusted to me if I would just rest and trust in Him? Of course. Did He really *need* me to do all that I was doing? No.

"You're right, God, I'm *not* that important," I admitted aloud. "I don't have to be everywhere doing what ultimately only You can do. You are God and I am not. And I do want to find that resting place."

I still boarded a plane the next morning for that media tour. But upon arriving at the hotel in Winnipeg, I took a long swim and stared up at a ceiling that was painted blue with glow-in-the-dark stars and thanked God that in the midst of the flurry, He was breathing rest into my life. I went back to the hotel room and went to sleep early, dreaming of a life of rest that I would find when I returned home. And I promised the Lord that from that day on, true rest and worship would be a priority in my life.

God has only blessed since.

In Matthew 11:28, Jesus says, "Come to me, all you who are weary and burdened and I will give you rest." "*This* is the resting place," Jesus is saying. "*I* am the resting place." Not the mountains, not the hotel, not the pool I was swimming in. Jesus is the resting place.

"Take my yoke upon you," Jesus continues, "and learn from me, for I am gentle and humble in heart, and you will find rest for your souls. For my yoke is easy, and my burden is light" (verse 29).

The burdens I take on myself are heavy—burdens like feeling I have to be everywhere to make sure things run right. Burdens like feeling the world will stop if I'm not in there running it.

Yet what does God call me to do? To love the Lord with all my heart, soul, mind, and strength.[37] To be still and know that He is God.[38] To act justly, love mercy, and walk humbly with my God.[39]

No, *His* burdens are not heavy. *Mine* are.

Jesus' own words to His Father in His prayer in John 17 set a beautiful example for me to follow: "I have finished the work You gave Me" (see verse 4). That's our only responsibility, isn't it? To finish the work *He* gives us. Not all the things we put upon ourselves. My, how restful our lives would suddenly be if we focused only on the work *He* gave us.

I love how, in the frantic times of Jesus' ministry, at the times when Jesus was "in demand"—He took time to break away and go to a lonely place. He knew His resting place was in communion with His Father. He knew that He needed to be rejuvenated and refreshed in His Father's presence in order to face the crowds again. We need that rejuvenating, too—to face our kids, to handle our responsibilities as women, to return to the office one more time, to slow down from a pace that is insane.

In His pursuing love, God will sometimes do whatever it takes to stop us in our tracks and make us receive and enjoy His rest.

This is the resting place…to get alone with God, our refuge and rest.

In Psalm 62:1, David said, "My soul finds *rest* in God alone," and in Psalm 91:1 he sang, "He who dwells in the shelter of the Most High will *rest* in the shadow of the Almighty." In Jeremiah 6:16, we are told to "stand at the crossroads and look; ask for the ancient paths, ask where the good way is, and walk in it, and you will *find rest* for your souls." I wonder why we're told that the rest will be found on the ancient path...the path that is rarely taken these days, the path less traveled. Could it be that the path of resting in Him is a route long forgotten, but a pathway wherein treasure still lies?

Isn't it interesting that God offers rest as a reward? He knows we need rest, and it is a treasure He wants to give to us. In His pursuing love, God will sometimes do whatever it takes to stop us in our tracks and make us receive and enjoy His rest. In Psalm 127:2 we're told, "He grants sleep to those he loves." Rest, refreshment, and rejuvenation is a gift from God to those who are trusting in Him.

❧   ❧   ❧

Not only is God our rest, but He is also our refuge—a place in which we can curl up and be secure. I think the two go hand in hand. When we are resting, we are secure. When we are secure, we are at rest. When my friend Tammi became stressed out about finances the year her pastor-husband took a job with a church that offered a salary that was next to nothing, she realized how very much she needed to find her resting place:

"I was afraid, feeling like the floor was snatched away from under my feet. My security was gone because I was depending on my husband's salary for security. We had just moved to a new state ten months earlier, just moved into a brand-new house six months earlier, and we were told that we would get $500 a month—that is, if the church was able to do so.

"I had trouble sleeping and eating and I wanted to cry all the time," Tammi recalls. "I didn't know how to cope with it. So I literally cried out to the Lord. I said, 'I don't have the trust in You, Lord, to get through this. You will have to provide for me that trust that I need.'"

Tammi was crying out for her resting place. And God, in His pursuing love, led her there...to His arms. Tammi learned much about her rest and refuge during those times of needing—and finally finding—her resting place.

"Once you learn to make Jesus your security, there isn't a thing that can shake you very hard. You may experience a tremor here and there, but that is not the same."

Today, Tammi says, "After ten years of witnessing God's constant provision, it would be a slap in His face to not trust Him, and I can't allow myself to do that to Him. I love Him too much."

Have *you* found that place in His arms where you are secure and at rest?

I have learned to look for a resting place—and find it—wherever I go. When I take the train back to my hometown in central California, my resting place is next to a window where I pray and write. When I stopped on my media tour at that hotel in Winnipeg, my resting place was that pool underneath the painted ceiling, where I swam and thanked God for the rest He was pouring into my life. When I rise each morning, my resting place is on the carpet with my back against my closed study door, where I play worship music, sing to Him, and let Him unveil the riches of His character from His Word. And in the stillness of the night, when there is much on my mind, my resting place is in Him, the only one who knows my heart and mind and has all the details of my life in His hands.

Where is your resting place? Is it in quietly trusting Him? In worshiping Him? In going away to a place to be with Him? Is it on your back patio in the quiet of early morning? Or is it on your pillow at night as you reflect on Him before falling off to sleep? If you don't have a resting place, cry out to God to show you where that place is and how to get there. Your soul needs it. And your God, in His pursuing love, is waiting to meet you there.

Finding
Your Resting Place

Prayerfully read the following verses and write what God might be telling you about leaning on Him as your rest and refuge:

Matthew 11:28-30—

Psalm 62:1-2—

Psalm 62:5-8—

Psalm 127:1-2—

When you think about your "resting place," what physical locations come to mind?

What spiritual states come to mind?

List one place you can retreat to—every day—that will allow you to get quiet and alone with God (even if just for a few moments) and regain your rest (be creative with this—your car, your closet, or the corner of your back yard are possible options).

My daily resting place: _____

Now, list a place you can go to maybe once a month to rejuvenate and regain a sense of renewed rest and trust in the Lord. (This could be your neighborhood park or a quiet restaurant or coffee shop—a place where you can shut out the noise or distractions and be alone with God.)

My monthly resting place: _____

᠅ ᠅ ᠅

A Prayer from the Heart

Thank You, Precious Lord, that Your burden is easy and Your load is light. Help me to know the difference between what I put on myself and what You lovingly place on me for service to You and my own good. Thank You for loving me enough to want to see me slow down and enjoy the rest that You wisely and lovingly hand me. I'm ready to recover my life, Lord...by resting in the shadow and shade of Your wings.

The Oasis That Quenches Your Thirst

16

*I*t was a long walk to the well in the scorching sun. But how fitting for *her.* She had always had to work long and hard for whatever it was she wanted. And still, she felt dried out and empty.

She wouldn't go to the well in the early morning when the other women of the village went. They'd just stare and look away. She was the one with the reputation. She was the one with no friends, only men. She was the outsider.

Who cares? She may have thought as she continued the trek to the well. When she arrived, she stopped. A man was sitting there at the well. She looked closer. A Jewish man! *What was* he *doing there?* she may have thought. *Should I leave and come back later? No, I walked all this way; he can leave!*

As she walked up to the well, Jesus apparently was expecting her.

Knew you'd come, He must have been thinking as she approached. In fact, He timed this meeting just right, having intentionally walked through Samaria, a place most Jews would've avoided, and sent His disciples into town so He could meet her alone.

As she approached, Jesus was getting ready to make history. He was readying Himself to say those now-famous words, "Please give me a drink."

"Why are *you* asking *me* for a drink?" she asked, shocked that not only would a man address her, but a Jewish man at that. Most Jews didn't want to associate with Samaritans. Most men wouldn't talk freely to a woman...especially a woman like her.

"If only you knew the gift God has for you and who I am, you would ask Me, and I would give you living water," Jesus answered, looking straight into her eyes.

"But sir, you don't have a rope or a bucket," she said, "and this is a very deep well. Where would you get this living water?"

But Jesus saw right through her words. Of course, to her, He had nothing to draw with, nothing to offer her that she hadn't heard or tried already. And yes, her well was deep...nothing had satisfied thus far. Did she think He was just another man offering her something to satisfy? Another empty trap?

Jesus spoke again: "People soon become thirsty again after drinking this water. But the water I give them takes away thirst altogether. It becomes a perpetual spring within them, giving them eternal life."

"Please, sir," she pleaded, "give me some of that water! Then I'll never be thirsty again, and I won't have to come here to haul water."

But Jesus wanted to get at her heart. "Come back with your husband."

"I don't have a husband," she said.

You're right! You don't have a husband," Jesus replied. "You have had five husbands, and you aren't even married to the man you're living with now."

Now the woman realized this man knew more than she had expected. "You must be a prophet," she said. She then changed the subject. "Why is it that you Jews insist that Jerusalem is the only place of worship, while we Samaritans claim it is here on this mountain?"

But Jesus didn't want to talk about religion. He wanted to talk about *her*—and what she was thirsting for.

He cut to the chase. He told her that worship is not about where it's done, but how it's done and to Whom: "Those who worship Him must do it out of their very being, their spirits, their true selves, in adoration" (John 4:23 THE MESSAGE).

"I know the Messiah will come—the one who is called Christ. When He comes, He will explain everything to us," she said, perhaps getting ready to end the conversation.

But that's exactly what Jesus wanted to talk about.

"I *am* the Messiah," He said clearly, watching her reaction.

I wish we knew what her immediate reaction was. At that moment, Jesus' disciples returned and the conversation was no longer private.

The woman turned to leave, without the well water she had come for. Perhaps she had forgotten why she came to the well in the first place. She had found *so much more*, and couldn't wait to get back home and tell everyone she knew.

We aren't told exactly what happened when she got home—only that Jesus had such a great impact on her that she told her whole village, "Come and meet a man who told me everything I ever did! Can this be the Messiah?" Her story was convincing enough that people came streaming from the village to meet him (John 4:30).

We're not told about the woman's life after that—if she married the man back home, or if she kicked him out. But because we're told that she left her water pot at the well, I tend to think she left her empty heart there as well. I think that as the hours and possibly days went on, she replayed in her mind over and over again the words that the Messiah had spoken to her. And I think she ended up ditching the guy back home. I mean, could she possibly go back and pick up with life where she had left it? I don't think so. After meeting God in the flesh, the epitome of what every man was created to be, how could any man—especially one who had never cared to marry her—compete? The guy back home was one of the six men she had in her life before Jesus. But Jesus offered her what she had really been looking for. And if that empty jar symbolized her empty heart, she left it there and went home filled and satisfied and not needing a container to try to find more.

Will we, too, after meeting Jesus, leave the empty watering can at the well and never thirst again?

Isn't it interesting that the God of detail—who cared to let us know that the woman left her watering can at the well—chose not to tell us how the story ended? Perhaps because He wants us to realize that the "rest of the story" is up to us—as we identify with that woman and make a choice about how to live our own life.

Will we, too, after meeting Jesus, leave the empty watering can at the well and never thirst again? Or will we go back to the way life was before, forgetting that we had encountered Living Water and we really have no need of anything else this world has to offer?

My friend Missie is one who left her pitcher at the well and lives on the Living Water that Christ offered her. After 17 years of marriage, her husband, who was active in the church and appeared to be very spiritual, left her for another woman.

"I could easily be an angry, bitter woman because he's taken so much from me," Missie says about her ex-husband. "But God has promised to be my provider, to supply all that I need. It's reassuring to know that He sees my beginning and end. I see only the present moment, but He can see how He will work this out for good and He has the power to get me there."

Missie readily talks about how Jesus meets her emotional needs, gives her strength beyond what she thought she had, and ministers to her in ways that are deeply personal.

"I remember feeling so lonely right after I moved here. I had no friends and I remember saying, 'God, I know I have you, but sometimes I need someone to touch, someone I can see right in front of me.'

"What did He do?" Missie laughed. "He brought more friends to me than I could handle."

Missie says not just any woman can find Jesus and lose the thirst for a man again. "You have to be in love with the Lord. If you're not in love with Him, you don't really know Him." Missie cultivates that deeply personal relationship with God by often dreaming of Him, instead of a man, as walking alongside her.

Missie is drawing water from the well that satisfies. She has found her oasis in the desert. She has found the Living Water that quenches any desire for any other kind of water.

I can relate. When I found Jesus to be *my* Living Water in the midst of some "dry" times in my marriage, He brought more harmony in the relationship between me and my husband than I thought was possible. And He showed me how He can sustain me even when I felt as if I had dried up.

Psalm 107:9 says God "satisfies the thirsty and fills the hungry with good things (NLT). In John 7:37-38, Jesus says, "If you are thirsty, come to me! If you believe in me, come and drink!" (NLT).

What an incredible offer! Have you accepted the Living Water that quenches your thirst and satisfies your soul? If so, how did it change *your* story?

$\mathscr{D}$rinking of the $\mathscr{L}$iving $\mathscr{W}$ater

When you think of what you truly need, physically, emotionally, and spiritually, how has God filled you and made you thirst no more?

Do you have that living water flowing from you? _____ If so, thank Him for it. If not, ask Him for it, believing He will supply all that you need.

According to John 7:37-39, what was Jesus referring to when He talked of "streams of living water" that would flow from within those who believed in Him?

Read Psalm 63:1 and write it here:

Make Psalm 143:6 your prayer this week (this would be a great verse to memorize, too!): "I spread out my hands to you; my soul thirsts for you like a parched land."

   ❧   ❧   ❧

A Prayer from the Heart

Lord Jesus, I reach out for You. I thirst for You as a parched land thirsts for rain. My soul pants for You like the deer pants for the water brooks. Be my Oasis in the desert of my life. Be the Living Water that flows up in me and leaves me filled, satisfied, and longing no more. Take my empty jar and heart, Lord God. I no longer need it now that I have found the Living Water of Your love.

The Patient One Who Watches and Waits

*D*an sat in his tent, eyes glazed over, as he held Debbie's letter in his hand. She was the one he wanted to marry. She was the one he was willing to wait for. Now it looked like he might never have her.

Stationed in Saudi Arabia, awaiting what would eventually be known as the Persian Gulf War, Dan had no idea if and when he would return home. But he held onto hopes that if he *did* return home, he would marry his Georgia girl. But Debbie's letter indicated she was taking a step backward from the relationship, seeing the time and distance between them as a sign they should call things off. Crushed by the news, but still aching with love for this girl, Dan realized there was nothing he could do to change her heart or mind. He turned his thoughts to prayers and decided to continue to wait anyway. Love sometimes means waiting. And waiting, for him, meant there was still hope.

That hope—not necessarily in Debbie, but in a God who might change her heart—kept Dan alive on the front lines of the ground war that later ensued. And upon Dan's arrival home, he found that Debbie's heart had, indeed, changed and their relationship resumed. A year later, they were married. Dan had been patient with the one he loved. And he never gave up hope.

Patience and hope are synonymous. When we continue to wait for something, it's as if we're saying, "I am hoping it will still happen." Our impatience, on the other hand, sometimes says, "This will *never* happen, so why wait?"

God's patience with us is filled with hope. Hope that we will respond. Hope that we will repent. Hope that we will return.

Jesus told a story in Luke 15 depicting His heavenly Father's patience, hope, and willingness to wait when it comes to us.

Jesus' story was of a father who had a rebellious son. This father must've been devastated the day his youngest son asked for his share of the inheritance. In Jewish culture, to ask for an inheritance early is like saying, "I wish you were dead." But the father gave to his youngest son what was rightfully his and watched with sorrow as the boy walked defiantly down the long road leading away from his family's home.

Finally, the boy thought as he got farther and farther from the gate. *Nobody's gonna tell me what to do anymore. I've got a life of my own now. I answer to no one. And the first thing I'm doin' is gettin' out of this wretched town.*

He got out of town...and a little out of his mind as well. He was determined to live high on the hog—until he sank lower than the pigs. By spending every last dime that he had, he ended up a homeless beggar, fighting pigs at a trough to get a bite to eat. He had nothing left. No money. No integrity. No excuses. He had not only ruined his name, but his family's as well. Finally, he realized his circumstances couldn't get any worse and he'd be better off returning home and living in shame as his father's slave.

It must have been a long, dreary walk home for the wayward young man. And by the time his father's house was in sight, the foolish son couldn't even lift his head. But as he humbly walked up the road toward home, something wonderful happened.

His father had been watching for him.

The same man who had been wronged by his young son's insulting request and foolish behavior had been eagerly watching and waiting. Perhaps every day he looked down that long road, remembering that painful day his son left and wondering if today would be the wonderful day he would return. This time, he saw the lonely figure from a distance and—*could it be? Is it…him? Is it…really…finally him?*

"It is!"

The excited father thought nothing of his dignity as a Jewish man, his reputation as a father to hold his son accountable, his family name that needed to be restored. He thought only of holding his son in his arms again. And so he ran. He picked up his tunic to his knees and ran to meet his son! And when he reached his astonished son, he threw his arms around his neck and smothered his sweaty, smelly body in kisses. His son had come home! Tears of joy welled up in the father's eyes, and when he finally managed to speak, he called for a party! His son was home, and this was cause for celebration. No lectures. No stern looks of disapproval. No demands for an explanation. Not even some "working through the pain." Just a party—in his son's honor!

🌿 🌿 🌿

We, as women, have ways of taking our "goods" from God and going our way. We sometimes get the idea we can live on our own and answer to no one. And yet, when we really think about it, there never was a reason to leave in the first place.

We've all had times when we've lived a little and learned a lot. And we often find during those times that we're worse off than we dreamed we would be. When we remember how warm and comfortable it was to be in our Father's presence, it's His love that compels us to return home. He knows all about what we've done while we wandered on our own, just as the father had heard of his son's bad choices and misfortune. But God waits, arms open wide, to welcome you back home. No questions. No lectures. No punishment. Just forgiveness and acceptance. And a celebration—in your honor! Your return to your Father is cause for a party. And you're the guest of honor.

God never gets tired of giving us a second chance.

"But I've disappointed Him so many times," you may say. Haven't we all? Yet His forgiveness and patience still stand.

The Bible says, "Why do you say...my way is hidden from the LORD? Do you not know? Have you not heard? The LORD is the everlasting God, the Creator of the ends of the earth. He will not grow tired or weary and his understanding no one can fathom" (Isaiah 40:27-28).

He knows what you've done; it wasn't hidden from His sight. But unlike people, who give us just so many chances and then lose patience with us altogether, God never gets tired of giving us a second chance. He "does not become weary or tired" of us, our problems, our pain.

How can that be? Because His understanding—both the things He knows about us and the things He loves about us—is unfathomable. Go figure. He just loves us.

God's pursuing love sometimes hunts us down; other times it waits for our return. It follows us like a gentle blowing and woos us back into His arms. The Bible says love, in its purest sense, "bears all things, believes all things, hopes all things, endures all things" (1 Corinthians 13:7 NASB). Because God truly loves you, He continues to believe in you, continues to wait for you, and continues to hope that it is *your* face He will see coming up the road toward home.

Returning to His Love

Have you become a prodigal the Lord longs to see return? If so, picture your heavenly Father eagerly watching the road for you, waiting to receive you back. Then run to His loving, open arms. A celebration awaits!

Maybe you're not necessarily a prodigal, but you've left God in some way. Maybe you don't spend the time with Him that you used to. Maybe you're not as committed to His church, His people, His plans, His Word as He'd like you to be. Write out a prayer here, committing yourself to return to the Lord in this or these particular area(s):

Reflect on Psalm 119:76. Write it here as a reminder to have a heart that is constantly seeking to come back to the fold:

Is there something or someone for which or whom you have waited for so long that you have nearly given up hope? Ask the "God of hope" to give *you* the hope you need to continue to wait. The Bible says hope that is rooted in the Lord does not disappoint (Romans 5:5).

❦ ❦ ❦

A Prayer from the Heart

I have wandered away like a lost sheep; come and find me, Lord Jesus.[40] Bring me back to the fold where I need—and long—to be… back with You where Your loving-kindness abounds. Thank You for not giving up on me during my "wandering times." Let me feel the celebration that awaits in the embrace of Your wonderful, fatherly arms.

A Comforter Who Longs for Your Love

18

My daughter was only two years old when she first verbally expressed love and understanding for her Daddy.

Little Dana was watching her father mop the soaked carpet in the church hallway. He had dropped by the church building to pick up some things and found another septic tank overflow.

"What a mess," he said angrily, as he started the all-too-familiar chore of cleaning up. Dana asked a few questions and got short, curt replies. She heard a couple sighs of exasperation as her father, the pastor of the church, tried to keep from cursing up one side and down the other at the old, run-down building that took so much of his time in maintenance and repairs.

Despite his responses toward her, Dana's tiny heart went out to her frustrated Daddy. She crept up behind him while he was kneeling down on one knee wiping up the mess, reached her little hand onto his back and, while patting him, softly said, "I love you, Daddy."

Hugh stopped what he was doing, looked into the eyes of his only child, and smiled.

"Thank you, Dana," he said, this time much more gently. "Daddy needed that."

      ❧   ❧   ❧

How often we, as parents, express our love to our children. We do it on a daily basis, through our sacrifices for them, our provision for their needs, our rules and regulations, and our constant concern for their well-being. But rarely do

> *God takes special joy in the work He has done in our lives.*

they, especially while toddlers, take the initiative to return that expression of love. Many a child will respond with "I love you, too," given the proper prompting. But how many will offer it out of the blue?

God, as our heavenly parent, delights in our expressions of love toward Him as well. He gives us the very air we breathe. He grants us each day as a blessing in itself. He made us with our unique personalities and abilities. And He longs for us to recognize Him and the love He has shown to us. He doesn't *need* us to love Him. He is God and therefore needs nothing. But He *chooses* to want us and therefore desires our love in return.

What a concept! The Creator of the universe wants to get up close and personal with us!

But, what kind of enjoyment could He possibly find in you and I? Because we are His special creation,[41] God takes special joy in the work He has done in our lives. It makes Him even happier when He sees what we can do with His help, His provision, His love pushing us ahead.

Like any father, He longs to help His children. Like any mother, He longs to protect and nurture us. As our Creator, He made us, sustains us, and gives us all we need.

There may be days—particularly when we're experiencing difficulty and pain—when we don't *feel* His love. When we doubt His protection. When we wonder if He's really there at all. But those are the times when we can feel His presence the strongest—if we would focus not on the storm raging around us, but on the fact that our anchor is holding and our ship has not sunk.

When we're caught in the storms of life, could His love be evident in the inner strength He gives us to keep standing? Could His protection be seen in the fact that our circumstances could be far worse? Is it possible we could feel His presence if we turned our bitterness and self-pity into a search for comfort and peace? When we begin to see tough circumstances as a part of life and all the good things we have as blessings from above, our perspective changes and we begin to see less of ourselves and more of God and His deliverance.

Throughout the Bible, we see God's heart expressed to us and His longings for our love. In Luke 13:34, Jesus revealed the longings of God's heart when He said this to a group of people in Jerusalem—the same people who were rejecting Him: "O Jerusalem, Jerusalem...how often I have longed to gather your children together, as a hen gathers her chicks under her wings, but you were not willing!"

This is one of the saddest statements Jesus ever proclaimed: I came here for you, but you're looking for a Savior in someone else.

To the same extent my husband was comforted by little Dana's expression of love during a tense moment, he would have been hurt had he tried to comfort her and she rejected his embrace!

And that is what we do when Jesus longs for our love and we just won't have it.

God continues to pursue us, yet we often run. Many times we're determined to live our life our way, to make our own decisions. "I don't need anybody," we tell ourselves and others. Then something goes wrong. And we often blame God.

Yet He is the One who longed to gather us up under His wings and show us the way, provide us with peace, protect us from pain. And yet we wouldn't have it.

When we, like baby chicks, run from His fatherly protection, we find trouble lurking in every corner. It's strange that we would even want to run in the first place! Our heavenly Father longs for us to be under His wings. But when we continually reject Him and run away from His reach, we say, in effect, "I will not have it." So God came after us, through the sacrifice of His Son, and provided a way for us to be with Him after all. And those who respond to this love He "adopts" into His family (see Romans 8:14-17).

Think about it. God wanted to gather us together, but we would not have it. So He went out and got us. Love found a way.

Like a mother hen seeking to gather together her scattered chicks, God continues to pursue us, seeking to calm our confusion, put our lives in order, bring us back to where He can reach us. He pursues and pursues. How long will He pursue *you*?

Responding to His Call

Can you recall a time in your life when you felt God's love pulling you toward Him? Describe the experience:

Parents long to hear affirmations of love from their children. Won't you tell your heavenly Father how much you love Him in spite of whatever has happened to make you feel temporarily "unloved"? Write your letter to God here:

Like a baby chick out on its own, you are vulnerable to the attacks of this world, outside the safe haven of your heavenly Father's arms. What would it take for you to simply run back to the protection of His wings?

Reflect on Psalm 91:1-4. What have you come to know those wings and feathers to be like?

❧   ❧   ❧

A Prayer from the Heart

Thank You, Lord Jesus, for wanting to gather me under Your wings and calm my confusion and comfort my heart. I'm sorry for the times I would not welcome You because I thought someone or something else would take better care of me. Hide me in the shelter of Your wings and don't let me wander away from Your protective care again. Next to You is truly where I long to be.

A Loving Daddy Who Made You His Child

Melissa was 12 years old when her father died. Since that time she has felt a tremendous emptiness.

"The only way I can describe it is that everything I was at that time was placed on a rug. That rug was safe to me; it was my foundation. When my dad passed away, that rug was ripped out from underneath me and everything I knew was turned upside down. Through the years I've noticed that because of that one event in my life, I have had a very difficult time trusting that God would come through for me."

Yet God has gone out of His way to be a Daddy to Melissa.

"I have found that no matter what I do to not trust God, He still comes through for me, and then I feel enormously guilty that I could not just trust Him. I get worried, stressed, and uncomfortable and then WHAMMO! He shows up and I am amazed. I feel that God is trying to show me that He *can* be trusted, even when I feel He cannot."

Melissa's experience is not unique.

"I think when you are missing a father figure or you lack a relationship with your earthly father, it is very hard to build a relationship with God because you have nothing to compare it to," she said.

How God's heart must ache at the truth of Melissa's statement. God's intended pictures of His love for us—how a husband loves his wife, how a father treats his child—have so often been clouded and confused in our sin-plagued world. The mirrors He created for us to see His love have cracked and left a distorted picture. Yet He still found a way to make sure we know about His Fatherly love.

I find no more precious picture than the one He paints in His Word about our adoption story. Perhaps He knew that many of us would need this reminder that He did, in fact, want to make us His children, regardless of the cost.

Romans 8:15 says that when we accept Christ as our Lord and Savior, "We have been given the spirit of adoption" (NASB). God is our adopted Father. Now, that doesn't mean He ended up being stuck with us. We weren't an accident. We weren't unplanned children. He came after each one of us and made us His own.

There's a saying in our culture that "we're *all* God's children." But that's not true. We're all God's *creation*, but we are not all His children. If we were, He wouldn't have needed to adopt us. Each of us, although we came into this world looking like innocent babies, have been sinners since conception (see Psalm 51:5). And that made us children, the Bible says, of the father of lies, Satan (John 8:44). But God wouldn't settle for that. He wanted us to be His. He was determined to take us off the road toward destruction and set us on the path toward life, giving us Himself as the Father we could grow up to trust and imitate. He found a way to "legally" pull us out of our plight and make us His own. He *adopted* us.

My friend, Christi, who has been alone much of her adult life, recently decided to adopt an orphan from China, a baby girl. She started a process that took about two-and-a-half years and involved filling out forms, interviews, home studies, letters of recommendation, and waiting. Then she had to have her fingerprints taken, fill out more paperwork, have more interviews, and experience more waiting. Then she had to secure a loan for the tremendous cost of adopting a child interna-

> *When we hear the redemption story, it should make us feel so special, so very wanted, so extremely loved.*

tionally. Finally, a picture arrived. She then had to let the agency know if she wanted that particular child based on the picture and statistics. Christi excitedly wrote back and said, "Yes, this is the child I've prayed for." Once this was confirmed, she had to get a passport, take shots for foreign travel, and then wait for travel orders. When she finally got her travel dates, she booked the plane flight and when the day came, she and her mother boarded the long flight to China. When their plane finally touched down in China, Christi had to go through customs, attend meetings, meet with officials, sign more documents, and take a tour of China.

Finally, the moment she'd been waiting for arrived. She was handed her new baby girl, who by that time, was a year old. And that baby, in that instant, became hers.

When Christi brought home her little bundle, I couldn't help but think that someday, when little Paige hears the story of all the trouble, all the pain, and all the red tape her mother went through to rescue her, she would feel so special, so very wanted, so extremely loved.

You and I have heard the story of what our adopted Father went through to get us. But instead of going through red tape, He went through the red blood of His precious Son. It cost God far more than thousands of dollars to get us as His children. It cost Him the life and death of His only Son—on a brutal cross so we could be called children of God, so He could rescue us and call us His own. When we hear the redemption story, it should make us feel so special, so very wanted, so extremely loved.

God's Word tells us that we've been given the spirit of adoption so that we can cry out "Abba"—the Aramaic word for "Papa" or "Daddy"—the first word a child utters when she learns to speak. (We'd like to think our children first said "mama," but linguists have proven it is much easier for a child to utter the "b" in *abba* or "d" in *dadda* or "p" in *papa*, than the "m" in *mama*.)

Jennifer remembers, as a little girl, looking up at her father and thinking he could do anything. "He could fix anything—any problem and any scratches or boo boos," she said. "I was very blessed as a child. Now that I'm all grown up, I know my father is human and has his flaws, just like me. But the best part of the relationship I have had with my earthly father has strengthened the most important relationship in my life, the relationship with my heavenly Father."

When Jennifer took a Bible class I taught a couple years ago, I asked her and the rest of the women to think about the name by which they have come to know God personally. Jennifer's response, which she shared after class, was that she has come to know God as her "Daddy."

"I've always thought of myself as 'Daddy's girl.' I belong to Him," she said. Jennifer explained that when she prays, she mostly looks up, picturing her heavenly Father's face looking down at her lovingly, ready to provide all that she needs. That is the way she went to her earthly daddy for help, and that is the way she now looks to her heavenly Daddy for help. "I lift my face up to Him, like I'm that little girl again seeking my father's attention and help."

Jennifer later shared this poem with me that she wrote about her heavenly Daddy:

> My Daddy is the King of kings, the Creator of Life, the One I adore.
> My Daddy is my Hero.
> My Daddy is tireless, fearless and brave.
> My Daddy knows my dreams, my thoughts, my fears and my flaws.
> My Daddy carries and comforts me.
> He hears me when I cry.
> My Daddy truly knows best.
> He clothes the field in flowers and gives me rainbows.
> My Daddy concentrates on me, and the plans He has for me.
> My Daddy gives me purpose, joy and love.
> My Daddy is patient and generous.

He makes the sacrifice, takes my pain, my sin,
He bears it with grace and makes me new again.
My Daddy loves me so completely He came back
    for me.
My Daddy has given me hope and freedom.
My Daddy, my Perfect Hero.

Do you know your Daddy in heaven like that? Like a kind Father who is bent on doing everything He can to help His little girl? If so, you are blessed. You may have enjoyed a similar relationship with your earthly father, in which you could call him Daddy and, in having that, You were given a glimpse of the kind of relationship that your heavenly Father wants to share with you. But if you did not have that kind of relationship with your father, your Father in heaven wants to more than make up for that now by letting you call *Him* Daddy.

Gretchen was raised in a strong Mormon family in the Southern Bible Belt. When she was 23, she accepted Christ as her personal Savior, causing a lot of tension in her family.

"My father rarely, if ever, would talk to me," Gretchen recalls. At one point we had a huge fight about what the truth was and my role in the family. After that, I was devastated. My real Father, God, touched me and taught me that I need only *His* love and acceptance in my life. Once I believed Him and cared what He thought above what my earthly father thought, then suddenly I no longer was hurt by the actions of my family. Because I no longer *need* the love of my family for inner fulfillment, I am able to build a relationship with them that is built on my unconditional love of them, not on my need for acceptance from them."

Gretchen was able to break free from the pain and bondage of needing her father's love and acceptance by looking to the unconditional love and acceptance that comes from her heavenly Father—the One whom she can now, through her relationship with Him, call Daddy.

Do you find yourself in the bondage of needing a father's love and acceptance? Do you feel that hole in your heart that's been reserved for the Daddy you've always wanted? You can fill that hole now...with the One who has been waiting—and longing—for you to call *Him* Daddy.

Looking Up to Our Daddy

What images or memories of life with your father have positively or negatively affected your relationship with God?

Write out words that describe what you have always wanted in a Daddy:

Now, put a check mark next to the words that can be used to describe your heavenly Father. (For an extra blessing, use a concordance to find verses that mention these characteristics of your heavenly Father. Then write the reference to those verses next to your descriptive words. This can be a guide to come back to later when you need a "Daddy Refresher Course.")

Replace the word *Father* with *Daddy* in each of these verses and write them out. Then recite them back to your heavenly Father. He loves to hear your praise and adoration:

Psalm 2:7—

Psalm 68:5—

Matthew 5:16—

Matthew 6:26—

2 Corinthians 6:18—

A Prayer from the Heart

Abba, Daddy, how did You know? You must have looked through time and seen how very important it would be to me to feel I belonged to someone strong and loving, caring and capable. What tenderness You have shown me to point out so clearly in Your Word that not only am I Yours, but You have come after me like a Determined Daddy to pull me out of my plight. Thank You for always being there...for doing whatever it took to make me Your own. It is so wonderful to know I was not an accident, not an unplanned child, but a premeditated, clearly calculated, and fully planned child of You. My soul sings at the thought of being Your little girl. May Your soul sing, as well, to hear me call You Daddy.

The Source of Peace That Calms Your Soul

When Dana was just 18 months old, she woke up from a nap one day with a mysterious bruise on her forehead. She didn't seem bothered by it, but *I* sure was. It was the tenth unexplained bruise I had found on her body in the last two days. When I called the doctor and was told to bring Dana in immediately for some tests, I was concerned. But when the doctor, after reviewing the tests, instructed me to take Dana to the cancer/leukemia ward of a children's hospital to see one of the best blood specialists in the country, and said I should plan to spend several days there, I knew we were facing something *big*.

As my husband drove the 60 miles to the Loma Linda Children's Hospital in Southern California, Dana slept in her car seat and I stared out the window, praying that the Lord would carry us through the uncertain days ahead. Somehow it was comforting to know that none of this took Him by surprise.

Upon arrival at the hospital, I numbly filled out all the applications for financial aid and state medical assistance that we were told we would need. A nurse looked at the application, taking note of my pastor-husband's salary, and gently warned us that Dana's possible medical condition could ruin us financially. She instructed us to apply for any and all financial assistance that was available. Again, I reminded myself that God was sovereign and none of this was taking Him by surprise.

For the next three days, Dana underwent a series of blood tests and blood glucose injections to bring her blood platelet count up to normal. For some reason, she was quickly losing the number of blood platelets in her body, which made her extremely vulnerable to bruising and to coma or death if she were to bump her head and cause bleeding on the brain. The blood specialist seeing Dana wanted to do a bone marrow test to rule out cancer or leukemia and to see if her condition was chronic. He was hesitant to predict whether she would experience a normal recovery (which takes six months to three years, on the average) or have a chronic condition in which she would need to be hospitalized on weekends for treatment throughout her lifetime.

I surrendered to that and prayed, "Lord, You are the only One who can hold me now...it's just You and me."

The first two nights at the hospital, nurses woke Dana every two hours by injecting a needle into her veins. We were told she would need a bone marrow test on Monday to determine the severity of her situation. But on Sunday morning, while my husband was back at our church preaching a sermon 60 miles away, a nurse walked into the room and said, "The doctor's here and he's ready to do that test now."

For a few seconds, I panicked. My husband had promised he'd be with me when Dana was having the test, but now he wouldn't be able to get here in time! And because church had already started back home, and there wasn't a way to notify anyone, my friends wouldn't know to be praying at this moment. Before I knew it, they had whisked Dana into the surgical room and closed the door behind them. I was left alone in the hallway with my only baby girl behind the other side of the door, about to render part of her spine in a test to see if she had cancer.

"O Lord Jesus," I cried and sunk to my knees, against the wall. "Little Dana is in Your hands. You are her God and my God...and we so need You right now. Please surround us with Your peace and Your presence."

It was then that I realized that the timing of this surgery, again, did not take God by surprise. He knew exactly when the procedure would take place, and exactly where I would be when it happened. And He chose for me to be alone with Him. I surrendered to that and prayed, "Lord, You are the only One who can hold me now...it's just You and me."

There was something very precious in those moments that followed—those moments in which only God could be there for me. Looking back at that half hour of my life, I realize now that He didn't want me to share that moment with anyone but Him. It was *our* time together. That, to me, is so precious.

I don't remember it being a whole 25 minutes that I sat on the floor with the Lord out in the hallway while Dana was on the other side of the door, but I do remember feeling God's peace as if I were being carried up and away from that situation. It was clearly a peace that my husband couldn't have provided if he had been there, and a peace that my friends could not have given had they been present. It was a peace that could come only from the One who authors peace.

The next morning we learned that Dana did not have cancer or leukemia or a blood or cell disorder. She had suffered a rare reaction to an antibiotic that had attacked her own blood platelets. The blood glucose injections she'd been given during the two previous days had worked to signal her body to stop the attack on her immune system and her blood count was now back to normal. She was released four days earlier than antici- pated and had a complete and immediate recovery. The doctor said he'd never seen a child recover from this con- dition as quickly as Dana did. In addition, financial aid came in from everywhere—there were even agencies standing by to pick up whatever our health insurance or state medical insurance didn't cover. The Author of Peace worked out every last detail, even the cost of our cafeteria meals and the overpriced diapers Dana had used at the hospital.

Looking back on that situation, I realize God was showing me something very special about His peace in a time of uncertainty. He came through as Dana's Gentle Healer, as our Financial Provider, and as the Source of Peace that passes all understanding.

🌢 🌢 🌢

When Jesus left this earth, He told His disciples He would leave His peace with them for troubled times: "I am leaving you with a gift—peace of mind and heart. And the peace I give isn't like the peace the world gives. So don't be troubled or afraid" (John 14:27 NLT).

When Jesus says He leaves us *His* peace, we are getting something that is not of this world. How appropriate that Jesus—a man of incredible peace—is the One who offers it to us. This God-Man demonstrated unexplainable peace while He walked this earth and endured far more than we ever will. He displayed peace under pressure from the mobs that wanted to kill Him. He demonstrated peace in the Garden of Gethsemane when His prayers were interrupted and He was arrested by Roman soldiers. He stood silently during a mock trial in which He was falsely accused, and He displayed peace in the courtyard when He was brutally beaten and whipped. This mysterious peace kept Him from yelling bitterly at His accusers and sending the powers of heaven to destroy the crowds, and He died in dignity on a cross while experiencing excruciating pain. So, when Jesus promised to give us His peace, we can know that we have an unworldly peace that is more than we could ever need.

We are also told in God's Word that "the peace of God, which transcends all understanding, will guard your hearts and your minds in Christ Jesus" (Philippians 4:7).

I've experienced that peace that is "far more wonderful than the human mind can understand."[42] Although I wouldn't want to revisit the circumstances in which I experienced that peace, I have missed that wonderful sense of God's presence, which was so very evident during my time with Jesus there on the hospital floor.

Have you experienced the peace that transcends all understanding? You can, my friend. The God who pursues your heart longs to give you what is His.

Praising Him for His Peace

Insert your name into the following promise from Jesus: "Peace I leave with _____; My peace I give to _____. I do not give to _____ as the world gives" (John 14:27). (You may want to highlight this verse in your Bible as a reminder of the peace God gives to you.)

Reflect on Philippians 4:6-7 and write it here in your own words:

Read the following psalms and note particular truths that can bring peace and comfort to you:

Psalm 91—

Psalm 116—

Psalm 121—

Here's an acronym that may help you. To be at peace means to be:

P atient with God's timing
E ncouraged by His promises
A ssured of His control
C omforted by His presence
E xpecting His deliverance

❧ ❧ ❧

A Prayer from the Heart

Jehovah Shalom, You are the Lord, my Peace. How grateful I am that You know me from the inside out and there is nothing that comes my way that takes You by surprise. I rest in the knowledge that You are all-knowing, all-powerful, and all-capable with the details of my life. Thank You for going before me and experiencing struggles in this life so You can capably help me through with the peace You have. Lord, may I live in Your peace, showing others that I have something that is of another world simply because I know the Author and Source of peace, who can calm the raging storm.

The Romantic Who Shares His Heart with You

*W*henever I see the sun rise or a rose at dawn, I hear, 'I love you,'" said one of my friends recently. "Whenever I look up at the stars or think that He is the reason my cells are held together, I am awestruck. Whenever I see a flower in bloom I hear Him say, 'I made this for you.' Sometimes it's the little things that mean the most."

Those little things can be big things when it comes to recognizing a God who pursues our hearts.

Judi formerly had a job that required her to spend three to four hours a day driving (or sometimes "parking") on the Southern California freeways. One day, while sitting in traffic and being very frustrated, she remembered a sermon her pastor had preached about how—at times of frustration—we should look for signs that God loves us in order to remember that, ultimately, He is in control. So because she liked sunflowers, she decided that each time she saw one, she would consciously remember God's love for her.

Judi recalls that through that sermon, "a seed was planted in my mind," and from that moment on, she became aware of sunflowers all around her—in television commercials, on billboards, and along the freeway, sometimes even in the center divider. On one particular morning, as she was at a crossroads in her relationship with God and having a hard time trusting Him to do some things she knew He wanted her to do, she hit stop-traffic on the freeway. Irritated all the more, she exited the freeway and took some surface streets. She then came around a bend and there was an *entire field* of sunflowers!

"God knew what I was going through," Judi says. "He understood my humanity and my fear and He loved me unconditionally anyway. I pulled to the side of the road (by that sunflower patch) and resolved the issue with Him right then and there."

There was another time when Judi felt overwhelmed by the romance of God's love for her. She had planned to wrap up her church's women's retreat by giving a closing talk to about 30 women. Although she knew the women, the thought of speaking before them terrified her. She ended up preparing a message, but felt she didn't have an "opener" in which she could share from her heart. The morning of her talk, she walked slowly up to the podium, trusting God would give her *something* to say as an introduction. When she opened her folder of notes, she was startled to see a five-inch plastic stem with three sunflowers on it! She didn't remember telling anyone at her church her "sunflower story" and couldn't figure out how it could have been placed in her folder. Standing there speechless for a moment, she lifted up the sunflowers and shared her sunflower story to the women as the opener to her talk.

Since then, sunflowers have popped up in the most unexpected of places as gentle reminders to her of God's love and His capable control of her life.

"I do realize that in many cases, all those sunflowers were there all along—just waiting for me to recognize them, kind of like God's outstretched arms of love," Judi says. "But I also know that He has drawn my attention to them consistently, and that in some cases, I believe, He has put them there just for me, for that moment when I so desperately need to be reminded of His unfailing love."

How does God communicate His heart to you? Through a sunset He paints in the sky on your drive home? Through a double-ended rainbow that sings to you of His promises? Through timely words of Scripture that jump off the page and penetrate your heart?

Although God has a million ways to show you through His creation that He loves you, the most romantic aspect of God's love, I believe, is the way He connects our hearts with His by showing us His plans and His purposes through His Word and prayer.

In his *Created to Be God's Friend Workbook,* author Henry Blackaby says, "Any person in covenant with God sees things others do not; he hears things others do not hear; and his heart knows things others do not know."[43]

I began to sense this after my husband and I committed to praying on a weekly basis with four other couples from our church. As we met together to pray for our church's finances, future, and obedience to God, we began to see how God directed our group's hearts and minds to begin praying for the same things. We started seeing things others who weren't in the prayer circle didn't see, and started connecting things we'd heard to things we'd prayed for earlier. Life became very exciting as we realized God's heart was beginning to connect with ours during prayer.

During my times of communion with God, He sometimes reveals how He wants me to pray for others and His church. Other times He reveals deeper aspects of His character that apparently He wants me to see. And sometimes the result of that communion with Him is simply a greater awareness of His love through the beauty of His creation all around me.

When Jesus' disciples asked Him why He frequently spoke in stories and riddles to the people, Jesus replied, "You have been permitted to understand the secrets of the Kingdom of Heaven, but others have not" (Matthew 13:11 NLT). He explained that those who were open to His teaching would be given more understanding and insight. But those who had little or no desire to understand Him, would not understand at all. Then Jesus told His disciples, "Blessed are your eyes, because they see; and your ears, because they hear" (Mathew 13:16 NLT).

I want to be one of those with eyes to see the ways that God communicates to His people, to see the displays of His character, His wonders, and His ways. And I want Him to know He can trust me with eyes that will be looking for demonstrations of His love and ears that will be listening for His gentle whispers and instruction.

There were times I used to envy my husband for being able to pull wonderful nuggets of truth and deep insights out of the Bible. Why wasn't it as easy for me? Little did I realize then that the difference was the level of intimacy he had developed in his relationship with God. When I finally came to the point in my life when I really started focusing my time and energy into prayer and reading God's Word (in other words, I was focusing on a *relationship* with God), my eyes became more open to the treasures of God's Word and the secrets on His heart. When we look at the lives of men and women in the Bible who had a more personal relationship with God, we see that these same people are the ones with whom God shared His heart.

For example, God singled out Abraham and told him He wanted to set apart a nation for Himself. Later, God told Abraham His plans to destroy the cities of Sodom and Gomorrah so that Abraham could intercede on behalf of the few righteous in that city. Years later, God tested Abraham's obedience when He called him to sacrifice his beloved son atop Mount Moriah. I can't help but think that, in addition to God wanting a man whose faith and obedience He could build a nation on, God also wanted at least one man in this world who would someday understand His own heart when His Son, Jesus, would be sacrificed atop Mount Calvary.

This God who knows your heart from the inside out wants you to know His heart as well.

Yes, God was looking for a man who would understand His heart.

Later in Scripture God calls His servant David a "man after my own heart" (Acts 13:22). I used to think that was simply because God saw David pursuing righteousness and trying to please Him. But there was more to it than that. David was also one whose heart took after God's heart. David was the kind of man who was angered by what angered God and broken by what broke God's heart.

Can you imagine having a heart that takes after God's? A heart that breaks at the things that break God's heart? A heart that rejoices at the things that make Him rejoice? The closer you grow in a relationship with Him, the more you will have that kind of heart.

This God who knows your heart from the inside out wants you to know His heart as well. But He won't burden you with it. Or offer it out of the blue. He will, however, stop at nothing to bring you into a closer awareness of who He is, if that is what you truly want.

Second Chronicles 16:9 says, "The eyes of the LORD run to and fro throughout the whole earth, to show Himself strong on behalf of those whose heart is loyal to Him." (NKJV). So it appears God is looking for a few good hearts so He can be strong on behalf of those people. Is God looking for a few because He only *wants* a few? No, because there *are so few* who are fully committed and loyal to Him. Of all the people who lived in the ancient Israel, we only read of a few—such as Abraham, Moses, David, and Mary—who experienced an extra-close connection with God. There was something about their humble hearts that got God's attention. I, too, want to experience that kind of relationship with God, don't you? I too want to be up close and personal with Him, more so than the average Christian. But for God to reveal His heart, I must be one who has eyes to see Him, ears to hear His voice, and a heart that is obedient and sensitive to His.

Jesus, after telling His disciples all that would happen to Him in the days to come, said, "I no longer call you servants, because a servant does not know his master's business. Instead, I have called you friends, for everything that I learned from my Father I have made known to you" (John 15:15).

When we are true friends with God, He reveals to us what's on His heart, as He did with Abraham and with Jesus' disciples. Will you take the time that is needed to develop a true trust in and friendship with the living God?

Exciting things happen when you develop eyes to see demonstrations of God's perfect love and ears to hear what God has to say. As God continues His search for a few good hearts that are loyal to Him, will you become one of them?

$\mathscr{C}$ultivating a $\mathscr{C}$onnecting $\mathscr{H}$eart

What are some ways that you see God's love for you in creation?

In His Word?

In the circumstances of life?

Read the following verses and take note of how you can cultivate a heart that is loyal to God so that when He searches the world for a few good hearts seeking Him, He will land on you:

1 Samuel 15:22—

Psalm 51:6,17—

Micah 6:8—

1 Thessalonians 5:15-16—

🌹 🌹 🌹

A Prayer from the Heart

Lord, who can dwell up close and be personal with You? I know that is what You desire of me, but I ask You to give me a desire for that closeness with You as well. Please open my eyes to see Your daily demonstrations of power and condition my ears to hear Your gentle whispers of love. I truly want to know what's on Your heart, and I know this means taking the time to listen...and realizing sometimes You will take a while to speak. May I never again be satisfied with just knowing *about* You. Starting today, Lord, I want to truly know *You*.

A Creator of Beauty Who Calls You His Poem

Susie felt she was anything but beautiful. For the first three years of her life, her family thought she was mentally retarded because collapsed tubes in her ears prevented her from hearing anything. But when Susie was sitting in the road one day and didn't respond to a honking car behind her, Susie's parents discovered her hearing problem and saw to it that she had an operation to restore her hearing. But even with her hearing restored, Susie was still kept on the outside of things. Family members continued to refer to her as "the retarded one."

"It was like I watched my family while I was growing up," Susie says. "I never participated; I was always on the outside looking in."

Needing to be noticed and longing to be loved, Susie fell prey to relatives who began to molest her at a young age. By the time she was 14, she was confused, hurt, and betrayed, and still longing for love. She asked Jesus into her heart at a summer church camp, and felt that her new life in Christ would certainly mean change. But shortly after, Susie fell in love with a man five years older than her and became pregnant. Even though her boyfriend planned to marry her so they could keep the baby, she listened to the lies of unwise friends who convinced her that having an abortion would be best for her and her fiancé. Susie had the child aborted and continued with her plans to marry the man. But when he cheated on her, she realized the only man she had ever trusted had betrayed her.

"I remember lying in bed and aching from the pain," Susie recalls. And then she heard the voice of Pursuing Love.

"It was as if God had said, 'I know the feeling. I've been betrayed by you many times.'"

From that moment on, Susie wanted to live for God alone. She got involved in a church youth group, got discipled in her faith, and went on a few youth missions trips. But in the midst of her pursuit for righteousness, she ended up being betrayed and sexually manipulated by a counterfeit spiritual mentor and his family. In spite of this new heartache, and betrayal, even by people who appeared to be close to God, she desired more of God, not less of Him. One evening she told herself the only way she could escape the pain and be with God was to die. Susie took two bottles of sleeping pills that night and prayed, "God, I don't want to ever wake up again."

But she did wake up—at 6:00 o'clock the next morning. Pursuing Love wouldn't let Susie go. God wouldn't let her destroy what He saw as an eventual masterpiece. He waited until Susie gave Him the canvas so He could paint something new.

Shortly after realizing not even she could take her life, Susie met Andy, a nonthreatening friend from church, with whom she opened up. Andy got Susie into counseling, arranged for her to move out of her threatening situation, and pulled her out of the pit she had been living in.

Susie began to read her Bible and memorize verses of hope and encouragement, such as Romans 8:28, which tells us that God causes *all things* (even the bad things) to work together for good to those who love Him. "All I had to do is love Him," Susie says, recalling her surprise at the condition on that promise. "Oh my goodness. All I ever wanted to do was love."

She also found encouragement from Psalm 27:13 that she would "see the goodness of the LORD in the land of the living." "Not in death, but while living!" Susie exclaimed. She considered that her promise: "I will get to see the love of the Lord and experience Him while I'm still living."

Through some counseling and God's constant pursuit of her heart, Susie is now freed to not have to worry about her past circumstances, mistakes, "baggage," or why certain things happened.

Susie often shares her story today, telling people her life is "horribly wonderful." Horrible things happened, such as childhood sexual abuse, making a decision to abort her child, experiencing betrayal from a trusted spiritual adviser. But God also delivered on His promise to work *all things* for good. Out of the bad situations, came the wonderful—a stable, dependable man who loves her, four sons whom she treasures, a sensitivity and compassion for women who struggle with the same issues she struggled with, a light to her once-tired eyes, and a joy that is unexplainable. Although Susie admits she still struggles with the temptation to spiral downward into depression, she exhibits a contagious joy to all around her. Everyone refers to Susie as the one who's always smiling, the one who laughs so easily, the one who lights up a room.

"That is God's Spirit in me," Susie says. "That is how He turned my horrible into wonderful. Because by nature, I'm not that way. My mind wants to choose depression every single day. But the Spirit of the Lord instead chooses joy."

How can one explain a life like Susie's? How could such horrible things happen to a little girl and a young woman who simply wanted more of God? The answers don't come easily. But we do live in a world that is wrought with sin and the evil intentions and manipulations of mankind. And life is about pain—with or without God. The promise, though, is that God will work the ugly things of this world and all its stain on us together for good and useful purposes in Him if we truly love and obey Him.

Ephesians 2:10 says, "We are God's masterpiece. He has created us anew in Christ Jesus, so that we can do the good things He planned for us long ago" (NLT). The Greek word for "masterpiece" or "workmanship" is *poeima*, from which we get our English word *poem*. We are God's poem—can you imagine that? He actually considers us His unique masterpiece that He is conforming to become an expression of who He is. Susie, though battered and bruised by bad choices and the circumstances of this world, became God's "work of art" as He displayed His grace and power in taking her—an insignificant, overlooked child, an abused teenager, a confused and manipulated young woman—and turning her into a loving wife and mother, a capable servant of God, and a source of light and joy to countless women.

No matter what has happened in your life, God can redeem it, restore it, and transform it into something breathtakingly beautiful.

Today, Susie says, "I feel privileged to feel that depth of love that I wonder if others ever get to feel." How can she say that? Because she is ever aware of how far God pulled her from the pit. And because she's been through God's beautification process, she now possesses the beauty of a smile even in bad circumstances, the beauty of a testimony to the goodness and grace of God, the beauty of a sensitivity she now has toward others—especially young girls who have been victimized sexually—and the beauty of a joy that lasts no matter what her circumstances.

What is Susie's secret? She gave God the canvas of her life—and the brush—and acknowledged His right to design whatever picture He wanted to paint.

You are God's work of art, too. No matter what has happened in your life, God can redeem it, restore it, and transform it into something breathtakingly beautiful.

When I talk to women about being God's poem and masterpiece, I sometimes wonder if they're thinking, *I am no masterpiece. I am the practice piece.*

Perhaps you feel as if God made a mistake with you and you'll always be the predecessor to the real thing—that woman over there who seems to shine and radiate what you only wish you could.

No, *you* are His masterpiece as well.

God often waits until we are done making a mess of our lives. Then He patiently asks, "Are you finished? Will you give Me the brush and let Me do what only I can do with your life?" Then He has an amazing way of wiping the canvas clean and starting over—and coming up with something we never thought was possible. Second Corinthians 5:17 says when we are in Christ we are "a new creation"—a new masterpiece, for His glory.

But what about the lingering consequences of a life gone bad? Although God forgives and forgets our sins and mistakes, I happen to believe that *we* don't forget them so we can use them as resources to minister to others. And there are some consequences we can't erase—but we can point to them as reminders of how far God was willing to go to redeem us.

My parents' divorce was not something God fixed and reversed although He had the brush in His hand while working on the canvas of my life. But He's used the colors that pain has brought into my life to give me a sensitivity toward other women and children who have suffered from divorce. That aspect of my life, although seen as bad at one time, has made my painting richer and my ministry more practical and useful to others.

How can *you* be God's work of art, His poem, His masterpiece? Hand Him the canvas of your life, and the brush as well, and let Him do the painting. But, don't dictate to Him what your picture should look like. Instead, let Him add the colors and brushstrokes that need to be there for the final breathtaking presentation. You'll be amazed at the beauty He can bring from the ashes in *your* life as well.

*Y*ielding to the *C*reator of *B*eauty

What are some talents and abilities you have that make you unique? List them here.

Can you recall painful situations in your life that have developed in you a sensitivity toward others? (That is part of your uniqueness and a glimpse of how you can minister to others and show God's beauty to others.) List here some ways you might be able to reflect God's beauty through the pain in your life:

Reflect on the following verses and, next to each one, record your thoughts or prayers about being His masterpiece:

Ecclesiastes 3:11—

Ephesians 2:10—

Philippians 1:6—

ε *ε* *ε*

A Prayer from the Heart

Thank You, God, that no one is beyond Your beautification process. Thank You that no matter what mess I've made of my life, You can raise up beauty from the ashes. Thank You that You still see me as one created to be perfect, spotless, and without blemish in Your sight. Were it not for Your creative potter's hand, I would have no hope. But You are truly an Artist of Transformation. Please show me how I can be a unique expression to this world of who You are…and what only You can do.

The Faithful Defender Who Pleads Your Case

*D*o you ever hear those voices? The ones that tell you that you're not really a child of God and it's all in your head? What about the voice that says, "Who are you to expect that God will give you something better than what you have right now?" Or, do you recall the accusations that hammer you for not following through on your pursuit of God and all He desires you to be?

You'd think there is a battle raging over your heart and mind.

You know what, my friend? There is.

For me the battle is a subtle feeling of despair that creeps in now and then as the enemy whispers his threats and taunts: "You are so pathetic. Do you actually think God is pleased with all of that? You're only doing it for yourself…. You call yourself a follower of Christ, yet your heart is so dark at times…. No one truly good has a critical spirit like yours…. Why would your child grow up to follow God after seeing an example like yours?" When these cold, harsh accusations are unleashed, the battle picks up in the heavenly realm:

"She is mine," the accuser says smugly from his corner of the demonic realm.

But then our Defender rises up and pleads our case.

"No, she is mine. I have purchased her with My blood. She has been crucified with Me and it is no longer she who lives, but I who live in her, and the life she now lives in the flesh, she lives by faith in Me—the Son of God who loves her and gave Himself for her" (Galatians 2:20).

The battle may rage for awhile, but ultimately, one side always wins.

"It is finished."

The words that won the case centuries ago still echo through the halls of heaven, causing the accuser to slink back in shame. Defeated again, he seeks another heart and mind to accuse.

The day Jesus Christ emerged from the tomb and "set the captives free," the day He took His seat at the right hand of His Father in heaven, was the day my victory—and yours—was sealed.

Case closed. Defendant goes free. Can you hear the bells of liberty?

Several years ago I sat in a courtroom in Orange County, California, as a reporter assigned to cover a day in the county court system. There was something dark and cold about that room. Something condemning. And it seemed to affect everyone. There was the lifeless look on the defendant's face. The judge who wanted to get down to business and seemed anxious to get home for the day. The stern bailiff just waiting for someone to make the wrong move. The nameless jurors who would determine the defendant's fate. When the verdict was finally read and the man was found guilty on all counts of drug-related charges, I was surprised to see that the defendant didn't even react. His face remained expressionless and he never lifted his eyes. Perhaps this was the life he had grown accustomed to. Guilty. Guilty. Guilty again. His eyes never came to life as he was led out of the room and back to his cell, where he would stay until he was transported to the county jail. I wondered, for a moment, what life would be like if I had no hope, no chance of a defense on my behalf, no reaction to being locked up and put away so that society would be safer.

I was relieved when the case was over and I could finally go home. As I walked out the front door of the courthouse, the light and warmth of the late afternoon sunshine hit my face and I breathed deeply. I looked down at my hands, free of cuffs. I looked up into the sky and wondered how long it had been since that defendant in the courtroom had felt true freedom.

Because of Jesus, the accusations are silenced, the doubting voices are stilled, the sentence is erased, the guilt is removed!

I never want to be in that man's place, I thought to myself. *I never want to have to stand trial and hear that I'm guilty and then face the sentence.*

Then I thought for a moment about what the place of judgment would like look like in God's kingdom. How will it feel to someday stand not before a mere human judge, but the Almighty God, who would pronounce my sentence for eternity?

I will never know, I realized as a smile came over my face and I skipped down the steps of the courthouse into the wide open plaza below. And my heart began to sing of my Defender...and the case He has already won for me. *It is finished.* Price paid. Debts cancelled. My heart set free.

Scripture tells us that "if anybody does sin...we have one who speaks to the Father in our defense—Jesus Christ, the Righteous One. He is the atoning sacrifice for our sins, and not only for ours but also for the sins of the whole world" (1 John 2:1-2). Because of Jesus, the accusations are silenced, the doubting voices are stilled, the sentence is erased, the guilt is removed!

I love the way the New Living Translation renders this verse: "My dear children, I am writing this to you so that you will not sin. But if you do sin, there is someone to plead for you before the Father. He is Jesus Christ, the one who pleases God completely. He is the sacrifice for our sins."

Now that's a pretty strong defense—the strongest we will ever need.

If God can take care of our most needed defense—the defense for our very souls—then surely He can take care of the other defenses we need, such as defense from the accusations of the enemy, and defense from unfair accusations from people. In Psalm 35:22-24, David, who was being unfairly accused, prayed this to his Mighty Defender: "O LORD, you know all about this. Do not stay silent. Don't abandon me now, O Lord. Wake up! Rise to my defense! Take up my case, my God, and my LORD. Declare me 'not guilty' O LORD my God, for You give justice" (NLT).

In her book *The Perfect Love*, Ruth Myers says, "How foolish to ever take on the burden of trying to make sure I am treated with the justice and mercy I think I deserve! Why complicate my life and drain away my energies when God Himself is looking out for my best interests as I simply do His will?"[44]

The Bible tells us, "if God is for us, who can be against us?" (Romans 8:31). In other words, if we have the Almighty on our side, how could we possibly need a stronger, more thorough defense? The Savior who died for our sins now stands at the right hand of the Most High God pleading for our case, rising up against any accusation made on account of one for whom His blood was spilled. That is love that pursues, love that defends, love that sings of our victory—in Him.

One of the psalmists in the Bible sang, "How blessed [or happy] are the people who know the *joyful sound!* O LORD, they walk in the light of Your countenance" (Psalm 89:15 NASB, emphasis added). Do you know "the joyful sound," and is it causing you to walk in the light of His presence? For me the joyful sound is the sound of my salvation, the sound of debts cancelled, sins forgiven, a heart set free. The next time those accusations start to bombard you, focus on the voice of your Defender. And listen closely—you just may hear the bells of liberty ringing on your behalf.

Living in His Freedom

To defend means to prove one blameless. Have you ever personally thanked God for how He has proven you blameless through His Son's work on the cross? If not, do that now.

Reflect on the following verses that speak of God as our Defense, Refuge, and Stronghold. Next to each verse, write a simple prayer thanking God for being your defense.

Isaiah 25:4—

Psalm 9:9—

Psalm 18:2—

Psalm 27:1—

Psalm 46:1—

A Prayer from the Heart

Lord, You are the Defense of my life, and a sure defense at that! How could I be in better hands? Thank You for not only defending me against the accusations of the enemy but for protecting me, as well, from the unfair accusations of men. Forgive me for feeling I must defend myself, when there could be no greater defense in my court than You. "In Your majesty ride forth victoriously in behalf of truth, humility and righteousness" (Psalm 45:4). Thank You that "the Eternal God is a dwelling place, and underneath are the everlasting arms" (Deuteronomy 33:27 NASB).

The Perfect Love You Long For

24

Claire was an upright woman with a good heart. She was a leader in her church. She was married to a godly man and had two beautiful children. But Claire was longing for a true connection with someone, and her husband was so very busy in his job.

Tim was passionate about the same things as Claire... and they talked many times at work about the way they saw God working in their individual lives. They were both vocal about their faith with others they worked with and they developed one mind about God and the Christian life. As their friendship grew, Claire sensed her heart longing for more from this man.

Claire knew the relationship that started so innocently, so righteously, had the potential to be dangerous, and she realized that even though she and Tim had done nothing that was at all wrong, an affair had begun in her heart and mind.

She fought the growing temptation to fantasize about him. She wanted to see him more and began to crave their conversations. One night she got up out of bed and went into her guest room and got painfully honest with God, crying out, "Lord, I want to be right in my heart...but he is so much of what I want and need right now. Is it wrong to want a man of strength and resolve? Is it wrong to desire a closer connection with one who is so like You?"

And then, most unexpectedly, God's love crashed through Claire's confusion and gently reeled her back in.

Claire, that strength and resolve that you see in him is Mine, God seemed to be saying to the hollow in her heart. *Those understanding eyes that acknowledge you and value what you say are Mine. That boldness and zealousness for the truth that you admire in him is really Mine. I have made Tim all that he is. And I am the One you truly seek.*

> Jesus was willing to minister to women in a time when, culturally and literally, no one gave them the time of day.

God reminded Claire that He is the one she really longed for—that her desires were rooted in what was right, but were running in the wrong direction.

Come to Me and experience all that I am, God seemed to say to her heart, *and you will not need to be swayed by one of Mine who merely, and unknowingly, shows you glimpses of Me.*

Realizing that her heart had responded to the things she loved about her Lord opened Claire's eyes to both the danger of transferring her love for God toward a man, and the realization that she could know joy—and not scandal—by redirecting her attention and passion toward the Lord.

Claire's attraction to Tim didn't suddenly stop, but ultimately it did shift wholly to her Lord and then to her husband. Today Claire is seeing in her husband the same things she once admired in Tim. "That is so exciting," she said. "And so is God's way of protecting me and pursuing my heart." Claire's heart is now determined to seek God for fulfillment, to stay in the arms of Irresistible Love.

"I can't tell you how much it means to me to know that God knew my intentions and gently rescued me from possibly dangerous actions," Claire told me about three months after her heartfelt dialogue with God. "He just wooed me back to Himself by showing me that all along it was characteristics of *Him* that I was admiring."

Have you ever thought about the male characteristics you're attracted to and how they might mirror the Ultimate Man—Jesus Christ? Jesus revealed His righteous anger when He confronted the religious leaders of His day and passionately said it like it was. He showed His strength and zeal for righteousness when He overthrew the temple tables. He showed self-confidence when He set aside cultural norms and asked the Samaritan woman at the well to give Him a drink. He displayed His masculine valor when He defended a woman for crying shamefully at His feet. He revealed the sensitivity and tenderness of His heart when He boldy but gently let a woman caught in adultery go free.

Jesus was willing to minister to women in a time when, culturally and literally, no one gave them the time of day. And it wasn't His physical appearance that attracted women to Him. Isaiah 53:2 tells us Jesus "had no beauty or majesty to attract us to Him, nothing in His appearance that we should desire Him." So, we can be certain it was His deep interest in their hearts that caused women like Mary and Martha of Bethany and Mary Magdalene to follow Him. It was the tough and tender, passionate and personal, commanding and comforting presence of God that these women—and all the people who found themselves drawn to Jesus—simply couldn't live without.

Have you, like Claire, longed for a closer connection with strength, compassion, tenderness, zeal? Then you are truly a woman. And your desires can run in a devastating direction or be corralled toward Christ, where they will reap lovely rewards. Your heart was made to respond positively—even eagerly—to a man who shows integrity and righteousness as he lives above reproach, to a man who mirrors in some way the Perfect Love you are destined to enjoy.

Won't you bring the misdirected desires of your heart and place them directly at God's feet? Won't you turn over to Him the secret places of your heart where your longings have hidden? Come now, surrender to Him the desires of your heart. And find, in that place of surrender, the Author of perfect, irresistible love.

$\mathscr{P}$ursuing $\mathscr{P}$erfect $\mathscr{L}$ove

What qualities have you longed for in a boyfriend, husband, or best friend?

Which of those character traits can you find in the God of the Scriptures?

Take some time to reflect on the secret places of your heart. Who dwells there? Honestly tell God about your private longings and ask Him to fill that place with Himself.

Give yourself something as a reminder of the One who pursues your heart. (A heart pendant, a special ring, a verse in the Bible printed out on nice paper.) When your heart starts to wander, have a verse handy that will help to steer you back on course. Some of these might help: Psalm 90:14; Psalm 118:9; Psalm 145:14-19; Isaiah 54:5.

$\approx$ $\approx$ $\approx$

A Prayer from the Heart

"All my longings lie open before You, O Lord; my sighing is not hidden from you" (Psalm 38:9). You truly are the Perfect Love and the One I must keep my eyes upon. Thank You for the demonstrations of who You are in the masculinity and might I see in godly men. But don't let me direct my longings toward man. You truly are the One I must seek above any other. Thank You for understanding what my heart desires are and for being all that I desire. Please make the psalmist's prayer my song as well:

> Satisfy [me] in the morning
> with your unfailing love,
> that [I] may sing for joy
> and be glad all [my] days
> (Psalm 90:14).

The Prince Who
Ransomed Your Heart

Only recently have I discovered why I love the Cinderella story so much. In a sense, it is the story of my life. And it may be the story of your life, too.

As we become young women, we, like Cinderella, may find ourselves orphaned and needy, perhaps the victims of a world—and lost loves—that have treated us badly. We find ourselves dressed in the rags of our own self-righteousness, and we hang onto a distant hope that out there somewhere exists a true love that will one day make things right. Then, when True Love finally appears, in all His splendor, and we find He wants us to be His princess and live happily ever after in heaven, we come to realize what real love and beauty is all about.

In the 1998 movie *Ever After*, the Cinderella story is portrayed by a young peasant woman named Danielle who disguises herself as a courtier and ends up capturing the heart of the crown prince of France. But knowing that she could never marry a man of his prominence—because he is royalty and she is a mere peasant—she ends up, ashamedly, being taken into bondage by a wicked man who intends to manipulate and abuse her for the rest of her days. Yet in one of the closing scenes, as she is walking in rags away from the dungeon where she was held, the prince comes to meet her. She recognizes him, but then looks down, embarrassed at how she looks, wondering why the prince would even want to talk to her knowing now that she is only a slave.

But then in a touching scene, the prince gets down on one knee, removes the ragged, dirty shoe from the young woman's foot, and slips on a glass slipper—a shoe representing royalty—as he confesses his love for her.

"You are my match in every way," the prince says. "And I would feel like a king if you, Danielle, would be my wife."

Tears well up in the woman's eyes as she covers her face and cries. Nodding yes, she throws her arms around the prince's neck and the delight in his eyes shines through as he picks her up and twirls her around. The love song plays in the background and the scene swirls around, showing the old dungeon behind them and the promise of a life of love, riches, and royalty in front of them.

Why do scenes like that often bring tears to our eyes? Why do we love stories about the prince who rescued the peasant girl and made her his bride? Because we yearn for something better, for real happiness. God created us to live in a perfect world, and because of our fallen state, there is a void in our hearts that longs for a return to what God created us to be.

We have a God who has come for our hearts to pull us out of that dungeon where we've been trapped by our sin and the evils of this world and to make us His own. Like the prince who knelt before his beloved and confessed his love, Jesus—the royal one—got on His knees for you when He went to the cross to purchase you as His bride. He humbled Himself for you—the one in rags, the one who was in prison to the bondage of this world, the one who was a slave to sin. He did it because He made you and He loves you.

> *"I have loved you with an everlasting love; I have drawn you with loving-kindness" (Jeremiah 31:3).*

I love the way the prince, in the movie, says, "You are my match in every way." Danielle didn't feel like his match. She was dressed in rags, and he was dressed as a prince. She was of the lowest social class; He was royalty. You and I were not God's match, either. God is the perfect sinless One, and we were covered in the dirt of sin and dressed in the rags of self-righteousness. And yet Jesus went to the cross to exchange our sin for His holiness so that He could bridge the gap between us and make us His bride. Jesus thoroughly and completely did what was necessary to make us His match.

You are that woman He has pursued from the ends of the earth and back. He was willing to go to the grave and back to get you for His own. Only one man could do that for you—and only one Man did—2,000 years ago. Why?

He spells out the reason in Scripture: "I have loved you with an everlasting love; I have drawn you with loving-kindness" (Jeremiah 31:3). In Isaiah 62:12 He calls us "Sought After" and in Isaiah 49:15 He says we are unforgettable. It is words like these that we often hear used to describe a woman who is much loved, a woman who is greatly pursued.

Jesus explained to His followers that He came to this earth not to be praised as royalty, but to "give his life as a ransom for many" (Matthew 20:28). And in Hebrews 9:15, we are told that Christ is the mediator who has "died as a ransom to set them free." He went to the cross to set us free. We have hearts that are now free to serve our Creator, our Redeemer, our Prince, the One who set us free.

Every display of romance we see in this world, every heartbeat that resonates with something true and right, every bit of pleasure that stems from something truly good is a mere glimpse of what God came to bring—what He wants us to experience with Him.

Cheryl, a 31-year-old woman with a history of bad relationships, had given up on love when Keith entered her life and pursued her heart. A painter who always had masking tape on hand, Keith would leave Cheryl messages spelled out in masking tape letters. One time he "taped" a note on her car windshield saying, "I love you this much..." and wrapped the remainder of the tape around her car several times. The expressions of his love and devotion just wouldn't stop. Cheryl married him four months later. But the one thing that attracted Cheryl to Keith the most was his tender heart for God. Keith's "romantic ways" were just evidence that he knew "The Author of Romance" and had hoped to win Cheryl's heart much like God had years earlier.

Wisely, Cheryl continues to see God first in all that Keith does for her: "Keith's love for me has been nearly as consistent as God's love has. Even though I say and do the wrong things, my husband is still there, just like God. Keith's persuasive pursuit of my heart shows me how God pursues my heart."

Praise God for the glimpses of romance we see here on earth that remind us that He is up to something bigger and better. But if you haven't experienced romance like that, don't despair, my friend. What God has in store for you will literally sweep you off your feet and make the romance of this world pale in comparison.

A friend of mine who teaches college was leading a class discussion one day on the concept of love as portrayed by the media. "What is true love, anyway?" he asked the students. "Ladies, what is it that would steal your heart away?"

One young woman said: "I can't think of anything more romantic than if a man was willing to die for me."

Before the teacher had a chance to respond, a young man in the back of the class blurted out, "One Man already has." The hushed silence that followed told my friend that the point was well taken.

The next time you begin to feel like one who is not worthy of being pursued, remember who you *really* are. You are the one who caught His eye. You are the one for whom Christ died so He could get you as His own. You are the slave girl who became the princess, the bride of the Prince of Peace. You are the woman who will someday wear a crown (that you will gladly hand to Him) and will live by His side happily ever after—all because God ransomed your heart and made you His own.

Surrendering to Our Prince

List the titles of two or three of your favorite love stories (these could be fairy tales, movies, or actual stories in history). Now pause for a few minutes and think about the correlations between God's love for you and the plots of the stories you like. You may find that what you love most about those stories is that it is your story of how God pursued you.

You've read about 25 ways that God pursues your heart. Which methods of His pursuit mean the most to you and why?

He fashioned you in love
He promises to never leave
He longs for your return to His arms
He promises to return for you
He always finds a way to provide for you
He offers you true rest
He turns the bitter to sweet
He shares with you His heart
He gives You a new life
He calls you His poem
He comforts and consoles
He ransomed your heart

By which names have *you* come to know God personally?

My Protector	My Hero
The Fulfiller of Dreams	My Rescuer
My Provider	My Oasis in the Desert
The Restorer of all Things	My Comforter
My Redeemer	Loving Daddy
Encouraging Friend	My Faithful Defender
Heavenly Husband	My Prince

❧ ❧ ❧

A Prayer from the Heart

Lord Jesus, there is no greater love than what You demonstrated in coming after me, dying in my place, and rising again to take me away. How breathtaking to realize the great price You were willing to pay to ransom my heart and make me Your own. Thank You for *all* the ways You have pursued my heart from the ends of the earth and back. May I live from this day forward knowing I am a woman much loved, a woman ever aware of the God who stopped at nothing to pursue my heart.

Giving Him Your Heart

To be cleansed of your sin and receive salvation in Christ, you must be in a relationship with Jesus Christ, God's Son, the only bridge between your sin and a holy God. A relationship with God, and that cleansing, begins when you surrender your heart to Him:

1. Admit you are a sinner by nature and there is nothing you can do on your own to make up for that sin in the eyes of a holy God (Romans 3:23).

2. Accept the sacrifice that God provided—the death of His righteous and sinless Son, Jesus, on the cross on your behalf—in order to bring you into communion with Him.

3. Enter into a love relationship with God, through Jesus, as a response to His love and forgiveness toward you. (For more on developing and maintaining an intimate relationship with God, see my

book *Letting God Meet Your Emotional Needs*, Harvest House Publishers.)

4. Surrender to God your right to yourself and acknowledge His right to carry out His plans for you and to mold you, shape you, and transform you for His pleasure.

5. Find a pastor or women's ministry director at a Bible-teaching church in your area or a trusted Christian friend and tell him or her of your decision to surrender your life to Christ. They will want to pray for you and get you the support and resources you need to grow in your new relationship with Jesus.

Notes

1. Jeremiah 31:3; Isaiah 54:6-7.
2. Ruth Myers, *The Perfect Love* (Colorado Springs, CO: Waterbrook Press, 1998), p. 124.
3. Psalm 18:4-19.
4. Psalm 56:8 NASB.
5. Psalm 147:3.
6. Matthew 10:30.
7. John Eldredge, *The Journey of Desire* (Nashville, TN: Thomas Nelson Publishers, 2000), p. 14.
8. Psalm 16:1 THE MESSAGE.
9. Prior to Genesis 17:15, Scripture identifies her as Sarai. God later changed her name to Sarah (17:15). For clarity, she is identified in this book as Sarah.
10. Matthew 19:26; Mark 10:27.
11. Luke 15:31.
12. Psalm 138:8 NKJV.
13. Psalm 50:10.
14. Philippians 4:19.
15. Isaiah 54:5.
16. Exodus 15:26.
17. Exodus 15:27.

18. Joshua 2:12-13.

19. Joshua 6:15-17,22-24.

20. First Kings 18–19:12.

21. Jeremiah 29:11.

22. My paraphrase of Matthew 11:28-30.

23. Psalm 65:9-11.

24. Psalm 68:19 in the New Living Translation says, "Praise the Lord; praise God our savior! For each day he carries us in his arms."

25. Myers, *The Perfect Love,* p. 147.

26. Psalm 68:5: "A father to the fatherless, a defender of widows, is god in his holy dwelling."

27. John 14:6: "Jesus answered, "I am the way and the truth and the life. No one comes to the Father except through me."

28. In Matthew 6:33, Jesus said, "Seek first his kingdom and his righteousness, and all these things will be given to you as well."

29. See Ephesians 1:13-14.

30. Tricia McCary Rhodes, *Taking Up Your Cross* (Minneapolis, MN: Bethany House Publishers, 2000).

31. This story is told in Exodus 14:29–15:21.

32. This story is found in Judges 7.

33. Psalm 18:9; 68:33.

34. 2 Kings 6:15-17.

35. Mark 15:38.

36. Psalm 18:1 The Message, emphasis added.

37. Matthew 22:37-39.

38. Psalm 46:10.

39. Micah 6:8.

40. Psalm 119:176 nlt.

41. Ephesians 2:10 in the New Living Translation says, "We are God's masterpiece...."

42. Philippians 4:7 nlt.

43. Henry Blackaby, *Created to Be God's Friend Workbook* (Nashville, TN: Thomas Nelson Publishers, 2000), p. 141.

44. Myers, *The Perfect Love,* p. 252.

Other Books by Cindi McMenamin

When Women Walk Alone

Every woman—whether she's single or married—has walked through the desert of loneliness. Whether you feel alone from being single, facing challenging life situations, or from being the spiritual head of your household, discover practical steps to finding support, transforming loneliness into spiritual growth, and turning your alone times into life-changing encounters with God.

Letting God Meet Your Emotional Needs

Do you long to have your emotional needs met, yet find that your husband or those close to you cannot always bring fulfillment to your life? Discover true intimacy with God in this book that shows how to draw closer to the Lover of your soul and find that He can, indeed, meet your deepest emotional needs.

An Invitation to Write

Cindi McMenamin has a passion for encouraging, inspiring, and motivating women to develop a more intimate relationship with God. If you would like to have Cindi speak to your group or you would like to share with Cindi how God has used *When God Pursues a Woman's Heart* in your life, write:

Cindi McMenamin
c/o Harvest House Publishers
990 Owen Loop North
Eugene, Oregon 97402
Email: cindispeaks@msn.com
Or, visit Cindi's website at www.cindispeaks.com

Books You Can Believe In™

HARVEST HOUSE PUBLISHERS

A Divine Invitation
by Steve McVey

"I want to be obsessed with Him so that the things that don't matter, won't matter. I want to be inwardly at rest." From that heart cry, McVey experienced an invitation into intimacy with God.

Breaking the Bondage of Legalism
by Neil Anderson, Rich Miller, and Paul Travis

Here's encouragement for defeated believers. The authors expose the trauma of legalism—shame, guilt, pride—and show how knowing who we are in Christ liberates us from trying to be "good enough for God."